Business Correspondence | 30

SECOND EDITION

Rosemary T. Fruehling
Associate Professor
County College of Morris
Dover, New Jersey

Sharon Bouchard
Adult Education Instructor
Hopkins Senior High School
Hopkins, Minnesota

GREGG DIVISION | McGRAW-HILL BOOK COMPANY
New York St. Louis Dallas San Francisco Auckland Düsseldorf Johannesburg Kuala Lumpur London Mexico Montreal New Delhi Panama Paris São Paulo Singapore Sydney Tokyo Toronto

Designer	Jorge Hernandez
Illustrator	Stan Tusan
Sponsoring Editor	Joseph Tinervia
Senior Editing Manager	Elizabeth Huffman
Editor	Gloria Schlein
Production Manager	Gary Whitcraft

BUSINESS CORRESPONDENCE / 30, Second Edition

2 3 4 5 6 7 8 9 0 VHVH 7 8 5 4 3 2 1 0 9 8 7 6

ISBN 0-07-022342-4

Preface

For most office workers, business correspondence is an important part of every workday. To answer requests, return materials, report information, thank customers, explain procedures—to perform their daily tasks, office workers must write letters, memos, and reports. And each time they write, they show others how well (or how poorly) they are doing their job. To join the office workers who do their job successfully, you must be able to write letters, memos, and reports that will get the desired results.

Business Correspondence/30, Second Edition, will help you write effective communications without making you memorize rules or formulas. This program will show you why each letter, memo, and report that you write is different from all the others, and it will show you how to deal with these differences in the writing you do. Throughout this program, you will have many opportunities to apply your writing skills.

In Chapter 1, "Planning Your Correspondence," you will learn how to plan a message that will reflect your careful consideration of the reader, your reason for writing, and so on. Chapter 2, "Putting Your Ideas Into Sentences," will discuss methods of writing sentences that express your ideas most effectively. In Chapter 3, "Paragraphing," you will learn to use paragraphs as signals that help your reader follow your message clearly. When properly constructed, your paragraphs will join your topics into a smooth, informative message.

Even the most informative message may not be read, however, if it does not attract and hold the reader's attention. Chapter 4, "Attracting and Holding the Reader's Attention," will show you how to keep your reader's full attention from beginning to end. Chapter 5, "Considering Your Reader," explains the techniques of writing messages from the reader's point of view. This chapter will teach you how to instill the "you" attitude in all your written messages. In Chapter 6, "Editing for a Positive Message," you will discover how to appeal to the basic needs and desires of your reader so that each message you write will be vivid and convincing—and will receive a positive reaction.

The general techniques presented in the first six chapters will be applied to specific types of business correspondence in Chapters 7 through 15. Chapter 7, "Writing Requests and Thank You's," will show you how to write successful letters and memos requesting materials, reservations, appointments, and so on. It will also present effective ways to express your thanks sincerely.

Chapter 8, "Answering Request Letters," will help you to reply to requests in a way that will maintain goodwill, as all correspondence should. Messages that are written *specifically* to build goodwill—for example, announcements, invitations, and letters of appreciation or congratulation—are covered in Chapter 9, "Promoting Goodwill." Chapter 10, "Selling by Mail," is very important because the techniques used in successful sales letters may be applied effectively to all other types of business correspondence. This chapter will explain the factors that motivate people to react favorably to some sales letters and negatively to others.

As a business worker, you may have to write—and answer—claim letters. Chapter 11, "Writing Problem-Solving Letters," will prepare you to write claim letters effectively and to answer claim letters tactfully, even when you must refuse the claim. In Chapter 12, "Applying for Credit," you will become familiar with the most common types of personal- and business-credit letters: namely, letters that ask for, grant, or refuse credit. People who abuse their credit privileges require special communications. Chapter 13, "Collecting Unpaid Accounts," presents some of the common methods of writing letters to notify customers that they are late and to convince them to pay their bills.

Two of the most important pieces of business correspondence that you may ever write are the résumé and the letter of application. Chapter 14, "Preparing Employment Letters and Résumés," offers a step-by-step approach to writing an effective résumé and letter of application. When you are on the job, you will probably write many reports for many different purposes. Chapter 15, "Preparing Reports," offers practical instruction on organizing information for the informal reports that you will write. It also outlines the general procedure for writing a formal report.

As you study each chapter in *Business Correspondence/30* and complete your writing assignments, be sure to use the Reference Section at the end of the book to check your punctuation, capitalization, number, and abbreviation style. The Reference Section also shows examples of the letter styles that are most widely used in business today.

ROSEMARY T. FRUEHLING
SHARON BOUCHARD

Contents

1

Planning Your Correspondence

Plan Ahead to Make a Good Impression

Since joining Bartlett Binders, Inc., a week ago, you have been attending the company's in-service orientation program. Most of your time has been spent becoming acquainted with company procedures and policies and getting to know your co-workers.

This morning you are assigned to work in the customer services section as a customer correspondent. Although your supervisor, Ms. Irene Laird, seems very friendly and helpful, she is busy this morning. She asks you to dig right in and check your incoming-mail basket. Upon doing so, you find the following letter from Mr. Keith Rodgers of the Acme Printing Company:

Dear Ms. Laird:

Is there an error in your August 13 Invoice 561-24? In your catalog, which we received 5 or 6 weeks ago, the price of your No. 17423 plastic spiral binders is listed at 4 cents each. The invoice accompanying the order, however, quotes them at 6 cents each.

Customers are already complaining about the high cost of these binders. We must clear up the discrepancy in cost before our present stock is exhausted.

Please investigate and let us know as soon as possible whether an error has been made.

Sincerely,

EXERCISE

In a copy of the catalog, you find the binders listed at 4 cents each. However, the first page of the catalog states, "Prices are subject to change without notice." In looking through the source materials in your desk, you find no updated price information for this product. Since this is your first writing assignment, you would, of course, like to make a good impression. You realize, though, that you cannot respond intelligently until you confirm the price of the binders. Your only alternative is to check with your supervisor, Ms. Laird. She informs you that the cost of plastic has increased and that your company has therefore had to raise the price of the binders to 6 cents. Using this information, draft a reply to Mr. Rodgers of the Acme Printing Company.

Unplanned Messages Waste Time. Let's analyze your reply:

1. How much time did you take to write the message to Mr. Rodgers? Can you afford to spend that much time on each piece of correspondence that you write?

2. Does your message assure Mr. Rodgers that you knew your subject well enough to provide him with a complete solution to his problem?
    a. Did you tell him that the correct price is 6 cents?
    b. Did you include an explanation for the price increase?
    c. Did you alert him to the notice in the catalog that "prices are subject to change without notice"?
    d. Did the tone of your letter reflect your understanding of the customer's situation?
3. Are the topics you discussed arranged in a forward-moving, smooth-flowing sequence? Although there is no one way to organize topics that are related to a particular subject, whatever method you use should make it easy for Mr. Rodgers to quickly and accurately follow your thinking.
4. Is your message geared to the needs and interests of Mr. Rodgers, or could it have been written to almost anyone with equal effectiveness? An effective business communication reflects the writer's total appreciation of the reader as a unique person; it also reflects the writer's understanding of the degree of formality or informality that is appropriate.
5. Does your message indicate that you had a specific purpose in writing? Although some communications have no purpose other than gaining the reader's goodwill, most also attempt to sell a product or service, settle a claim, or accomplish a similar objective. A message that has no clearly identifiable purpose represents a waste of time for both the writer and the reader.
6. Does your message make it clear that the reader must pay the full amount of the invoice?
7. Will your message assure the reader that you knew the extent of your authority concerning this matter?

Unplanned Messages Are Cold and Negative. Read the following reply to Mr. Rodgers. If you were Mr. Rodgers, how would you react to this message?

> **Dear Mr. Rodgers:**
>
> **Unfortunately, you are mistaken regarding the correct price of our No. 17423 plastic binders. If you had read the notice at the bottom of the first page of our catalog, you would have seen the**

following statement: "Prices are subject to change without notice." You must realize that escalating costs of production have to be absorbed in part by the consumer. Therefore, the price of the binders has been increased from 4 cents to 6 cents each. Since this increase was not known until after our catalog was printed, we had no way of getting this information to you before you placed your order.

The amount of the invoice is correct. Therefore, we will expect a check from you for the total amount of the invoice within 10 days.

Sincerely,

This message hardly creates a good impression of Bartlett Binders. The tone is cold and negative, and it implies that the customer is ignorant and has difficulty reading. Moreover, even if the writer had the authority, he or she should never write so offensive a statement as, "Therefore, we will expect a check from you for the total amount . . . within 10 days."

To make sure that your letters are effective and that they create a good impression of you and your firm, you must *plan* your letters before you write them.

I SEE THAT KEITH RODGERS HAS READ THE LETTER FROM BARTLETT BINDERS.

Plan Ahead to Write Effective Letters

The need for planning before writing cannot be overstated. Whether you are initiating or answering correspondence, you will always find it helpful to plan ahead by developing a written working outline. You will discover that planning ahead will provide considerable assurance that every letter, memo, report, or other communication that you write is not only worthwhile but also as effective as you can make it.

Answering Incoming Letters. When you are answering an incoming letter, you have a concrete source of information that you can consult as you:

1. State the purpose of your letter.
2. Determine what response, if any, you would like your reader to make.
3. Decide the main subject of your letter and the topics related to it that you will have to present and discuss in order to write a complete message. When replying to incoming correspondence, many successful writers simply underline or jot down in the margin the topics that will have to be covered.
4. Decide the best sequence for presenting and discussing the topics you have underlined or listed. After doing this, number or letter the topics in an informal outline form; then check to see that each topic is relevant—omit those that are not.
5. Consider your reader and, in every way possible, plan your message from the reader's point of view.

Following these steps, you might have outlined the reply to Mr. Rodgers like this:

1. Purpose: To explain to Mr. Rodgers that our Invoice 561-24 is correct.
2. Response desired: To have Mr. Rodgers accept the price increase—and our invoice—as fair and reasonable and to have him continue as our customer.

3–4. Subject: The price of plastic binders has been increased from 4 to 6 cents. Topics: ② Since March, we have absorbed two price increases from plastics manufacturers. ③ We had to pass along the third increase to our customers. ⑥ Our invoice is correct. ⑤ The price rise became effective on August 1. ① It's not listed in our catalog; that's why the invoice is confusing. ④ Because of such sudden increases from manufacturers, we state in our catalog that the prices listed are "subject to change." ⑦ If Bartlett explains this to its customers, they will better understand the reason for the price increase.

5. The reader, Mr. Rodgers, seems to be a reasonable person who is concerned about what appears to be a mistake. As a business worker, he will appreciate the fact that costs do increase. If we can show him that the invoice is correct, he will pay it; if we can convince him that the increase is justified, he will remain one of our good customers.

From an outline such as this, you might have written the following letter to Mr. Rodgers:

Dear Mr. Rodgers:

I can certainly understand the confusion regarding Invoice 561-24, especially since our catalog does list the price of No. 17423 plastic binders at 4 cents each.

During the past six months, we have had to absorb two price increases from plastics manufacturers. However, when we were informed of a third price rise, we simply had to pass along part of this increase to our customers. Because sudden increases from manufacturers sometimes occur, Mr. Rodgers, we have found it necessary to qualify our price quotations with a "subject to change" policy, as stated on page 1 of the catalog.

On August 1, we found it necessary to increase the price of the plastic spiral binders from 4 to 6 cents. Therefore, Invoice 561-24 is correctly stated.

Perhaps your customers will be more understanding if you explain this situation in terms of the increased costs in these inflationary times.

Sincerely,

This message creates a better impression of Bartlett Binders, Inc. Although Mr. Rodgers may not be overjoyed with the increased cost of the binders, he will understand that increases in costs must be absorbed by customers as well as by producers. The tone of this letter is formal and matter of fact but still cordial. It shows that the writer understands the scope of his or her authority and knows the subject. Also, the writer leaves no question in the reader's mind as to the correctness of the invoice.

Initiating Your Own Correspondence. When you are initiating correspondence, your outline should again include a complete statement of your purpose in writing, the response you want your reader to make, the subject of your message and the topics you will have to present and discuss, and a quick sketch—based on whatever information you can gain from sources that are available to you—of your reader. If you don't personally know your reader or if you have no ready sources of information about your reader—and you often will be writing under such circumstances—there's nothing you can do but use your best judgment in developing a sincere, personal quality.

EXERCISES

1. In your incoming mail today, you receive the following letter requesting your supervisor, Ms. Irene Laird, to be a guest speaker at a Lions Club banquet.

Dear Ms. Laird:

On behalf of the Lions Club, I would like to invite you to be our guest speaker at a banquet on April 10, 19—, at 8:40 p.m. It will be held at the Governor Morris in Morristown, New Jersey.

This banquet will end a three-day conference at which members from all districts within the state will have met to exchange ideas, ratify resolutions, and endorse new policy. Your address could present the need for civic and service projects that enhance community character through family participation.

Besides offering you an honorarium of $100, we will, of course, reimburse you for your travel expenses. If possible, please confirm by March 10.

Sincerely yours,

Andrew Countryman
State President

After checking with her about the speaking request, Ms. Laird tells you to accept the invitation. Using the following Planning Guide, develop an outline of the points you would have to consider in actually writing the reply.

PLANNING GUIDE

(1) State the *purpose* of your reply.

---

(2) State the immediate or long-range *response* you want your reader to make.

---

(3) State the *subject* of your message and list the *topics* that you will have to present and discuss.

---

(4) Number the *topics* in the order in which you will discuss them.

(5) Give a brief *description* of your reader.

---

2. Using the Planning Guide on the next page, develop a written working outline for one of the following:

a. An inquiry about the content of and the one-year subscription rate for *Career*, published by Smithson Publishing Company.

b. A request for information regarding admissions procedures and scholarship opportunities at the vocational-technical school or junior college in your area.
c. A request to a department store in your area for information about their credit application and payment policies.
d. A letter asking for a donation from a local business executive to help sponsor a Careers Day for the senior class in your school.

PLANNING GUIDE

(1) State the *purpose* of your message.

(2) State the immediate or long-range *response* you want your reader to make.

(3) State the *subject* of your message and list the *topics* that you will have to present and discuss.

(4) Number the *topics* in the order in which you will discuss them.

(5) Give a brief *description* of your reader.

2

Putting Your Ideas Into Sentences

In Chapter 1 you learned that in order to write a good letter, you must define the purpose of your message and you must consider your reader and plan your message from the reader's point of view.

Once you have defined the purpose of your letter and have outlined your main ideas, you will be ready to draft a response—to put your ideas into sentences. In this chapter, you will discover techniques that you can use to put your ideas into sentences and to make your sentences more effective.

Expressing Simple Sentences

In presenting your ideas, you may decide that the best procedure will be to present each of the points in your outline in a separate sentence. For example:

1. Will you please send me information about the admissions procedures for your school.
2. Will you also please send me a description of the scholarship opportunities available to high school graduates.

These examples show two ideas expressed in two simple sentences. Since each sentence contains one complete thought only, each can stand alone as an independent idea or an independent clause, as above. However, both sentences can also be combined into *one* complete sentence, as you will see in the discussion below.

Combining Ideas of Equal Importance

Two closely related ideas may be joined into one sentence in a number of different ways. For example, you may prefer to combine two simple sentences by using a comma plus *and:*

1. Will you please send me information about the admissions procedures for your school, and will you also please send me a description of the scholarship opportunities available to high school graduates.

The two ideas that were expressed in two simple sentences are now joined by a comma and *and* to form one compound sentence—one sentence with two independent clauses.

The same two ideas may be combined by using a semicolon to join the two independent clauses:

2. Will you please send me information about the admissions procedures for your school; will you also please send me a description of the scholarship opportunities available to high school graduates.

In this compound sentence, the independent clauses are joined by a semicolon instead of by a comma plus *and.*

The two ideas expressed in the original simple sentences may be expressed in a third way:

3. Will you please send me information about the admissions procedures for your school and a description of the scholarship opportunities available to high school graduates.

Unlike the compound sentences, the new sentence has only one independent clause; yet it combines the same two thoughts that were expressed in the two original simple sentences and in the two compound sentences. The last example contains one subject (*you*) and one verb (*will send*), just as the original simple sentences do. But the last example combines two ideas of equal importance, two requests, by compounding the objects, the things that are requested: "Will you please send me (1) information . . . and (2) a description . . . ."

Considering the alternatives illustrated above, which one do you think is best? Do you agree that the last sentence achieves the writer's objective in the fewest words?

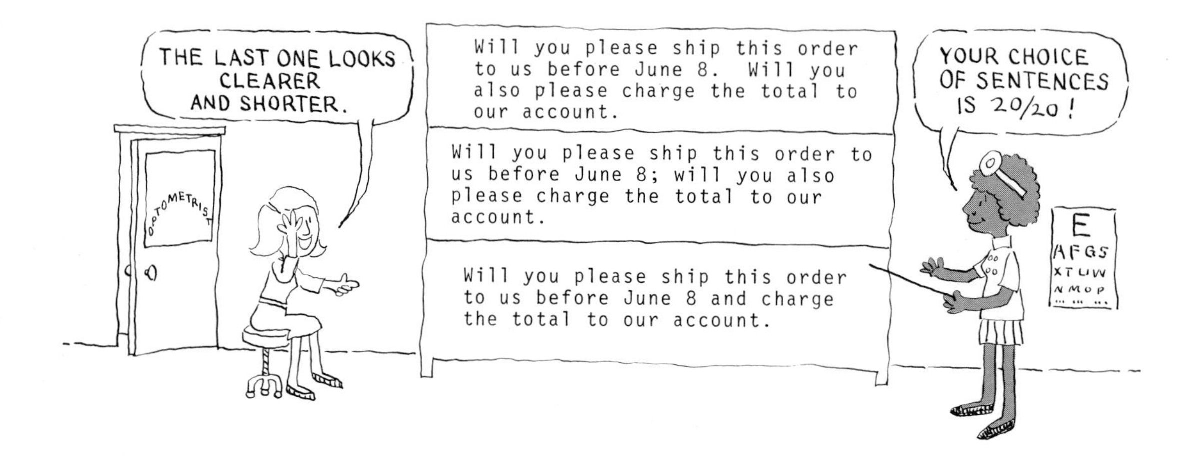

Combining Ideas of Unequal Importance

Suppose you wished to express in one sentence two or more ideas that you felt were closely related but *not* of equal importance. For example, consider the following related ideas:

1. I am planning to enter college next fall.
2. Will you please send me information about the admissions procedures for your school.
3. Will you please send me a description of the scholarship opportunities available to high school graduates.

In this particular case, you may wish to make the first of these ideas subordinate to the other two, because *I am planning to enter college next fall* is not as important as the requests for the admissions procedures and scholarship information. You may use a variety of devices to make sure that your reader recognizes that this idea is less important. Here are two examples:

1. Since I am planning to enter college next fall, will you please send me information about the admissions procedures for your school and a description of the scholarship opportunities available to high school graduates.

   The addition of the adverb *since* signals the reader that the first idea is less important than, or subordinate to, the two main ideas that follow. Notice that a comma is used to separate the dependent clause (which expresses the least important idea) from the independent clause (which expresses the main ideas).

2. Will you please send me information about the admissions procedures for your school and a description of the scholarship opportunities available to high school graduates because I am planning to enter college next fall.

   Notice the use of the adverb *because* to subordinate the minor idea; but in this case, the minor idea is put at the end of the sentence. This position de-emphasizes the subordinate idea further. (If you had positioned the dependent clause *because I am planning to enter college next fall* at the beginning of the sentence—another option—you would have put a comma after *fall*.)

Now consider joining two other ideas of unequal importance:

1. I am a new member of the club.
2. I look forward to the coming year under your leadership.

One of the two ideas, *a new member of the club,* may be subordinated in any of the following ways:

1. I, who am a new member of the club, look forward to the coming year under your leadership.

   Note the use of the pronoun *who* to introduce a dependent clause that subordinates the idea of being a new member. The use of the commas around the subordinate idea makes it clear that this clause provides further information about the subject *I*, information that is not necessary to either the meaning or the completeness of the sentence.

2. I, as a new member of the club, look forward to the coming year under your leadership.

   In this case, the preposition *as* introduces a phrase subordinating the idea of being a new member.

3. I, a new member of the club, look forward to the coming year under your leadership.

   The phrase *a new member of the club* further explains the subject *I* and is set off by commas because it is unnecessary to the meaning of the sentence. Here the subordinate idea is condensed to an appositive.

4. Being a new member of the club, I look forward to the coming year under your leadership.

The participial phrase *being a new member of the club* gives emphasis to the main idea, *I look forward to the coming year under your leadership.*

5. I, being a new member of the club, look forward to the coming year under your leadership.

   Note that here the participial phrase *being a new member of the club* has less emphasis.

The purpose of this discussion is to illustrate some of the many ways in which you can express your ideas and give them different degrees of emphasis. The more ways that you know how to combine ideas, the better you will be able to add interest and variety to your writing. Clauses, appositives, phrases, and so on, are devices that can be used to subordinate ideas. The more expert you become at using these devices, the better you will write.

EXERCISE

If necessary, rewrite the following sentences using the techniques of combining ideas.

1. Mr. Smith called you. He wanted to make an appointment.

____

____

2. You can buy Firestone tires at Steins. You can buy General tires at Wards.

____

____

3. Ms. Carson wrote the article. Mr. Jefferson will edit it.

____

____

4. I look forward to our meeting in March. I hope you will give some thought to the selection of a new agency.

5. We congratulate you on the completion of your project. We hope the enclosed description will encourage you to come to Des Moines.

6. New employees should understand the importance of cooperation. Experienced employees should too.

7. The Federal Reserve bank does not provide service to the general public. It provides service for its members.

8. Some of our staff members are very experienced. Most of them are trainees.

9. My instructions were to ship 211 catalogs to Boston. I need to know what has happened to this shipment.

10. Financial security need no longer be a dream. We hope you will stop in to learn how our Master Plan can solve your money worries.

____

____

____

Emphasizing Parts of Ideas

Both of the following sentences express the same idea, but note that each sentence emphasizes a different part of that idea:

1. Our attorney rejected the contract.
2. The contract was rejected by our attorney.

In the first sentence, the emphasis is on *attorney*, which is the subject of the sentence. The emphasis in the second sentence is on *contract*, the subject of that sentence. In the second sentence, *attorney* is no longer the subject and receives less emphasis.

Obviously, the position of the words in a sentence helps to determine how much emphasis each word receives. But the key to the above sentences is the verb used in each. The first sentence uses the active verb *rejected*; the second sentence uses the passive verb *was rejected*. Your choice of verb determines the emphasis that you will give to various parts of an idea.

By choosing an active or a passive verb, then, you can vary the emphasis on the parts of an idea. Consider the active sentence "Ms. O'Brien gave Mr. Evans the memo."

Ms. O'Brien is the subject, the doer of the action; *gave* is the action verb; *Mr. Evans* is the indirect object, the person to whom Ms. O'Brien gave the memo; and *memo* is the direct object, the thing that Ms. O'Brien gave to Mr. Evans.

To change the active sentence above to a passive sentence, do the following:

1. Make either the direct object or the indirect object the subject of the sentence.
2. Use a *being* verb (*am*, *is*, *are*, *was*, *were*, *be*, *been*, and *being*) before the main verb.
3. Use a past participle (a verb form that can be used with *has*, *have*, or *had*) as the main verb.
4. Use *by* with the subject.

By applying these four steps, you can change the active sentence to either of the following passive sentences:

1. The memo was given to Mr. Evans by Ms. O'Brien.

Note that *memo*, the direct object in the active sentence, is the subject of the passive sentence; the being verb *was* has been used with the past participle *given*; and *by* has been used with *Ms. O'Brien*, the subject or the doer of the action in the active sentence.

2. Mr. Evans was given the memo by Ms. O'Brien.

Mr. Evans, the indirect object in the active sentence, is the subject of this passive sentence. Also note the use of *by* with *Ms. O'Brien*.

Knowing how to create both active and passive sentences will allow you to choose which parts of an idea to emphasize. But unless there is a definite advantage to emphasizing the result or the receiver of an action instead of the doer, you should avoid using passive sentences. Active sentences are generally shorter and more direct.

When stating a formal policy or regulation, however, you may find a passive sentence preferable to an active one. For example: *Smoking in the stockroom is prohibited*. This passive sentence is more tactful and less antagonizing than an active sentence such as *I prohibit smoking in the stockroom*.

EXERCISES

1. Change the following active sentences to passive sentences.

a. We prefer brief, easy-to-read reports.

---

b. The management prohibits smoking in the auditorium.

---

c. The typist should type the manual.

d. You must surrender your credit card to the accounting office immediately.

e. The president of the college students' organization wrote the following letter to School and College Charms, Inc.

2. Change the following passive sentences to active sentences.

a. The Krause contract was returned by the file clerk.

b. You will be assigned a full-time assistant by the president.

c. A copy will be mailed to you today by the secretary.

d. The letter will be delivered by the mail carrier at noon.

e. The letters were transcribed by the secretaries, and the file copies were delivered to the Central Filing Department by a messenger.

f. Carol Bernstein was promoted to assistant manager by Mrs. Harnett.

g. The attaché case was found in the cafeteria by Elaine Hill and was returned to its owner by Elaine.

Controlling Sentence Length

A knowledge of the techniques discussed so far will help you control the length of your sentences. Research indicates that the most readable sentences are 15 to 20 words in length. Naturally, you may have some sentences of 10 words or less and some of 30 words.

Check the average length of your sentences and critically evaluate long sentences. Weigh each word. The busy reader will be annoyed with monotonous, wordy messages that camouflage the real meaning of your thoughts. In Chapter 5, you will learn some techniques that will help you to eliminate unnecessary words and phrases.

3

Paragraphing

You have studied techniques of developing sentences that will precisely convey single ideas or combinations of ideas to your reader. Now you are ready to place your sentences in a logical order and group them into paragraphs.

Separate Topics Into Paragraphs

A paragraph may be only one sentence long, but usually a paragraph contains several sentences—all related to the same topic. Thus, a paragraph may be defined as a group of sentences closely related to a specific topic.

There are several reasons for paragraphing. Grouping sentences into related topics helps to improve the general attractiveness of your business letter. Your business letter should invite reading; that is, it should look easy to read. Wide-enough margins, short- and medium-length paragraphs, and tabulated material—all help to make a letter inviting. Long, involved paragraphs are monotonous and forbidding.

The paragraph may also be used to highlight a statement or a question. The technique of enumerating points by paragraphing (treating each point as a separate paragraph) makes it easy for the reader to recognize and answer them.

The most important reason for paragraphing is to signal to your reader that you wish to begin the discussion of a new idea. By paragraphing, you make it easy for the reader to follow your thinking and for you to lead the reader through your message.

Just as you limit the number of ideas in a single sentence, so should you limit the number of sentences in a paragraph. Each paragraph should contain only those sentences that deal with one main topic.

EXERCISE

Read the following message. Then place the sentences in logical order and group them into paragraphs. Write the sentence numbers on the lines below. Use one line for each paragraph.

Dear Mr. Gardner:

(1) I am sorry that we cannot arrange to have you pay premiums on the monthly basis, as you asked, because monthly premiums must amount to at least $10. (2) Since your policy contains an Automatic Premium Loan Clause, we can arrange to have your premiums paid by loan provided that there is enough cash value in your policy. (3) Let us know if you want us to do this, won't you? (4) Then you can simply make repayments toward your loan and all will be in order. (5) However, this Automatic Premium Loan arrangement will, in effect, accomplish the same thing. (6) It will be a pleasure to take care of it for you.

Sincerely yours,

____

____

____

Let's analyze your solution:

1. In the first paragraph, did you group sentences (2) and (4) in that order?
2. Did you group sentences (1) and (5) to make your second paragraph?
3. Finally, did you group sentences (3) and (6) for your last paragraph?

Join Paragraphs With Transitions

One business writer who was asked how to write effective letters and reports said, "I grab the reader firmly by the hand, and I hang on until I'm finished." That's good advice. One way to "grab the reader firmly by the hand" and "hang on" is to bridge the gap between paragraphs by using connectors, or transitional expressions.

A good selection of linking words will allow your reader to follow your ideas not only from paragraph to paragraph but also from sentence to sentence. For example, in the preceding message to Mr. Gardner, note how the words *then* and *however* are used to join the sentences in the first two paragraphs.

In the following excerpt from *Business Communication: A Problem-Solving Approach,* by Roy W. Poe and Rosemary T. Fruehling (McGraw-Hill, 1973), note how the words *however* and *today* are used to link a paragraph to the preceding paragraph:

> **Many persons believe that new inventions are causing a shifting of jobs and unemployment. As each invention becomes popular, more workers lose their jobs. People also believe that when there is a depression, inventions should be registered with the government but not introduced until prosperity returns.**
>
> **However, others feel that progress should not be hindered. They believe that, in the long run, machines create more jobs than they destroy. For example, the discovery of electricity and the invention of the electric light threw many persons out of work, but on the other hand, thousands of newly trained workers were needed in the factories that manufactured electrical goods. The invention of the automobile threw carriage makers out of work, but eventually it caused many more people to be employed as automobile workers than had been previously employed as carriage makers.**
>
> **Today, skilled workers are learning how to perform other kinds of tasks. The industries created by the invention of the automobile, radio, motion picture, airplane, computer, and television have created, in turn, hundreds of thousands of jobs.**

Here are some of the common transitional expressions that will help your reader to follow your message:

To Show Cause and Effect

Accordingly | **As a result** | **Hence** | **Therefore**

Mr. Smith requested that we send copies of the letter to all new managers. Therefore, we made 50 extra copies.

To Show Exceptions to What Has Been Said

But	Even though	On the contrary	Otherwise
Conversely	However	On the other hand	Nevertheless

We can, as you suggested, be ready to leave by January 8. However, a move at that time will interrupt the children's school schedules.

I agree that Mary is more creative than Laura. On the other hand, Mary has no management experience.

To Indicate Time, Place, or Order in Relation to What Has Gone Before

Above all	Finally	In summary	Still
After all	First	Meanwhile	Then
Again	Further	Next	Too

Entering the foreign market is not as simple as it sounds. First, there is the language problem. Then, there is the matter of finding suitable personnel. Above all, we must face up to the fact that we will have to find suitable facilities.

To Introduce Examples

For example For instance Namely That is Such as

Many departments depend on this service; for example, the Accounting Department, the Personnel Department, and the Manufacturing Department.

Don't expect these transitional aids to perform miracles. Remember, if your ideas do not follow a logical sequence, no transitional device used will fool your reader. Just as the speaker who rambles on from one thought to another fails to present a clear message to his or her listener, so will you as a writer fail to present a clear message to your reader.

EXERCISE

Rewrite the following messages. Organize the sentences into a logical order and use transitional expressions to link sentences and paragraphs.

Dear Miss Lewis:

Please send us your booklets or pamphlets on fund-raising projects for small clubs, and I will present your ideas at our next meeting on Thursday, June 2, so that our committee can begin to reorganize our strategy of attack. Thus, we, too, are writing to you for advice. I have been asked to write to your company on behalf of our organization to ask you how we can improve the condition of our local fund-raising projects, which are not doing the job for our group that we think they should be. We would like to receive any of your suggestions that would be helpful to us in attempting to improve the condition of our problem. We feel your experience could help us get back on the right track. We know there must be a solution because we have heard about the successes other clubs have had after they have written to your company, the "ABC" Organizer, for advice.

Sincerely,

____

____

____

____

Dear Mr. Schmidt:

We will be very happy to answer any questions you might think of sometime later. We received your letter dated January 10 in which you ask for our advice concerning the buying and selling of securities. Answers to your questions in your January 10 letter may be found in our booklet for beginners in the stock market business of buying and selling securities. Our local consultant for your particular territory could also be of great help, we are sure. We are pleased to be able to be of help to you in any way possible, since that is the reason we are in business in today's busy world.

Cordially,

4

Attracting and Holding the Reader's Attention

Every writer likes to think that his or her message will absorb the reader's attention, but many messages fail to do so. If you assume that the reader is a busy person, you will understand why a powerful, forceful takeoff is needed to get your letter off the ground. In order to attract and hold the reader's attention, you must, from your first word, have something to say. Otherwise, your communication will be classified as "junk mail," mail that often gets thrown away before being read.

The Takeoff

If your takeoff is powerful and forceful and direct and interesting, your letter may be read carefully. A good way to ensure getting this attention is to open with a short, strong, definite statement. Make your opening short, but make it say something. Why not consider your first sentence of your first short paragraph your headline? Don't be afraid to have only two or three short sentences in your first paragraph. Actually, the fewer the better. In sales letters, the first paragraph is designed specifically to attract attention.

Remember that any reference to the date or to details of previous correspondence should be placed in a subordinate position. In other words, "Your January 12 letter was received yesterday" places the date of the previous correspondence in a predominant position; "Thank you for your letter of January 12 requesting 12 reams of our No. 16 white mimeograph paper" places the *thank you* and the actual sale in the predominant position and the date in the subordinate position.

You will ensure a powerful takeoff if you can describe action that was taken on your reader's behalf. This is always the most effective opening to a business communication. Action is impressive because it implies decision, and all of us are favorably impressed when our requests have been met. Note in the following examples how action in favor of the reader gets each message off the ground.

Dear Elizabeth:

Enclosed is our book, Success in College, which you requested in your letter of June 12. You will be pleased to know that this book is free to all high school Merit Scholarship winners.

Dear Mr. Yamato:

Thank you for inquiring about the possibility of becoming our sales representative in the Midwest. Every one of us in the Minneapolis office feels that you would make an excellent addition to our marketing team.

Another way to ensure strength and power in your opening sentence or paragraph is to avoid the use of participial expressions, except to subordinate an idea. Inexperienced writers who use participial expressions frequently may produce grammatically incorrect sentences. Notice how easily the following lengthy participial expression could be mistakenly considered a complete sentence: "Having reviewed your application for employment as a secretarial trainee." It is not, of course, a complete sentence.

Avoid all unnecessary preliminaries in your first sentence, and don't rehash what your reader already knows. For example, "Your order of January 10 reached my desk today" is obviously unnecessary. The reader realizes that you would not be responding if the order had not reached you, so why rehash?

Remember that the first sentence and the first paragraph are extremely important. Everything that follows builds from this opening. Be natural, and be yourself. Do not begin the first paragraph with the old-fashioned, pompous wordiness of yesteryear. Compare the following examples.

YESTERYEAR	TODAY
We desire herewith to acknowledge receipt of your letter of June 10. Heretofore, in the future, we wish to inform you that it will be unnecessary for you to notify us directly. From this instant it is with pleasure that we announce that notification of late payments may be made to the respective agent in your city.	**Thank you for your letter of June 10 notifying us of your late payment. For your convenience, all future notifications of late payments may be made directly to your agent, Mr. T. Jones.**

Obviously, the natural, up-to-date "Today" version is easier to read as well as easier to write. The first message is excessive; it marks the writer as pompous and behind the times. Acting natural and saying things as you would in a cordial conversation will get your letter off the ground with a powerful takeoff.

The Landing The landing, the last paragraph of your letter, should have a definite purpose. It should make it as easy as possible for the reader to take action or to accept what you have written. If you have considered your reader's point of view from the first word of your letter to the last, the reader will see how easy it is to do what you ask and how it will benefit him or her to do so. By enclosing an addressed envelope or postcard, you may readily stimulate action.

One of the serious errors that writers make is to ramble, and the last paragraph seems to be the frequent place for such rambling. Inexperienced writers are sometimes confused about how to end a letter. If your message has been conveyed, make a smooth landing. The reader doesn't expect you to be flowery or chatty. Just end the letter. And don't say "A speedy reply will be appreciated"!

The most ineffective of all closings is the participial ending. Ending your letter with, for example, "Trusting we shall hear from you soon" is weak and inconsequential. "Thanking you in advance" is even worse; it violates two rules of good letter writing. First, it is a participial expression; second, it is presumptuous because it assumes that the reader will grant what you ask.

Compare the "rough landings" on the left with the "smooth landings" on the right.

Looking forward to hearing from you soon, we are	**May we hear from you soon.**
Hoping that you will place your order with us soon	**Enclosed is an addressed postcard for ease in ordering.**
Trusting you will give this matter your immediate consideration	**Will you please act promptly on this request.**

By providing your reader with a powerful takeoff (a good opening paragraph) and a smooth landing (an effective closing paragraph), you will almost ensure that your reader's journey through your message will be a pleasant one.

The Best Approach

Although you have been given some suggestions for making an impact in your opening and closing paragraphs, there is really no "best" approach or formula. So much depends upon the relationship between you, the writer, and your reader. The following letters request the same thing, but they are written by two different people. The first writer is not a personal friend of the reader's, while the second writer is. Note that although both letters are effective, they do not have the same kinds of opening and closing paragraphs.

Dear Mr. Williams:

Will you please send me within the next two weeks the slides you used in your presentation to the Future Data Processors Association members on Saturday, May 9.

As you will remember, I asked you whether it would be possible for me to use these visual aids for a speech I have been asked to deliver to the Dover Lions Club on Friday, June 10. I truly appreciate your kind offer to lend these materials to me. You can be sure that I shall return them to you by registered mail on June 11.

Sincerely yours,

Dear Ted:

You were up to your usual good stage performance when you spoke to the Future Data Processors Association members last Saturday afternoon. It reminded me of your campaigning days at Rutgers when you were making your pitches to be elected to the Senate.

Ted, I appreciate your offer to let me use your slides for the speech I have been asked to give to the Lions Club on June 10. If at all possible, please send them before the end of this month.

You can count on my returning them to you the day after I use them. I'll let you know if I'm as big a hit as you were!

Cordially,

EXERCISES

1. Rewrite the following ineffective opening sentences and paragraphs.

a. In regard to the equipment, it is being shipped from New York today addressed to you at your office and have somebody there to receive the shipment because it must be signed for and will you be sure to acknowledge by letter to me.

b. In reply to your letter of July 1, we wish to advise you that an examination of our records shows that your policy is still in force.

c. Acknowledging receipt of your letter of January 10 in which you asked for a copy of *Good Listening*. We are glad to send you this copy.

d. Referring to your letter of April 2, we want to tell you that we find your new publication extremely interesting.

e. We desire herewith to acknowledge receipt of your esteemed favor of the 16th. We have given you credit for $69, the amount of the check enclosed.

f. With reference to your letter of June 12, we are unable to fill your order.

2. Correct the following ineffective closing sentences and paragraphs, or indicate when an unnecessary one has been used.

a. If you will send me a big order right away, it will help me win a prize in the contest that our company is conducting and you will receive merchandise that is superior in quality at no higher price than you have been paying to other dealers.

b. Hoping it will be possible for you to give us your decision on this matter by Friday, we are,

c. Assuring you in advance of our appreciation for your kind attention and hoping that we may have the opportunity to do the same.

d. Hoping you will return your broken glasses for credit as soon as possible.

e. Believing that you will find this booklet suitable, we beg to remain,

f. With best regards, I remain,

3. You are a correspondent in the credit section of a department store to which Carol Zanna has applied for a charge account. You are writing to an officer of the bank where Miss Zanna has a checking account. You want to know Miss Zanna's credit rating. Write your opening paragraph—and remember that this is a routine inquiry, since you do not know Miss Zanna personally.

____

____

____

____

____

4. You are writing a letter to Mr. Mark Pulaski, the personnel director of the Power-O-Peat Company, Seattle, Washington, to apply for the position of accounting trainee. You state your experience and qualifications. You know that he will be attending a convention in your hometown, Spokane. It would be very convenient if you could have an interview with him sometime during his stay in Spokane. Write your final paragraph, your request for action.

____

____

____

____

____

5. Indicate by a check mark which of the following is the best way to include a reference to the date of your reader's letter.

___**a.** This is in reply to your letter, dated April 22.

___**b.** Thank you for your interest in our advertising program, expressed in your letter of April 22.

___**c.** We are in receipt of your letter of April 22.

5

Considering Your Reader

After you have drafted your sentences and paragraphs and combined them to draft the first copy of your message, you will have to examine the message to make sure that it reflects a feeling for your reader and that it does not contain any jargon, unnecessary phrases, outmoded or overused words, and so on. As a beginner you may find it necessary to do lots of rewriting. After all, even experts don't always say it right the first time. Some outstanding authors find it necessary to rewrite their manuscripts many times. So be prepared to rewrite your message to make it effective and courteous.

Develop a Feeling for Your Reader

Please and *thank you* are words that suggest courtesy, but these words do not automatically ensure a proper display of respect, concern, consideration, and helpfulness. The intangible qualities of courtesy can best be achieved if you will remember that all correspondence must be written from the reader's point of view. The reader's point of view is really the "you" attitude or seeing things through the reader's eyes.

"I want to get a part-time selling job with your firm so that I may earn money to enroll at the University this fall" is certainly not considering the reader's point of view or using the "you" attitude.

"Will you please consider me for the part-time selling vacancy in your firm. I plan to attend the University this fall and need to earn money to pay for my college expenses" incorporates the word *please* and the word *you*. However, it still lacks the intangible qualities of courtesy which show that the reader's point of view has been considered.

Let us try to change the paragraph not only by adding a courteous *please* and using the word *you* but also by considering the reader. "Will you please consider my application for the part-time sales position with your firm. Since I plan to major in marketing and merchandising at the University this fall, you can be sure that I would be an enthusiastic trainee, eager to learn selling." A prospective employer will certainly be more impressed with the last illustration, because the writer has indicated how he or she would be an asset to the employer's firm.

To write effective communications, then, consider the reader's point of view. Always assume that your reader is a successful, extremely busy business executive—not too busy, however, to recognize the benefits or profits of hiring a promising applicant or sending the materials requested or replacing a defective product.

Unfortunately, you cannot inject the "you" attitude into your letters merely by substituting *you* and *your* for *I* and *we*, *my* and *our*, and so on. Consider the following two examples and notice that there is no magic in simply saying *you, you, you.*

Dear Mrs. Jones:

I'm sorry for the delay in shipping the Dubarry lipsticks. Since I want to make sure I send you exactly what you want, though, I'm holding up the order until I get more information.

Just indicate your shade selections on the enclosed card, and mail it to me today. As soon as I receive it, I will ship your order immediately. I'm happy to say that I have all shades in stock.

Sincerely,

Dear Mrs. Jones:

You failed to tell me what shades of Dubarry lipstick you wanted. As a result, you will not be able to have your order when you wanted it.

Will you please let me know exactly what shades you want. You may refer to your spring catalog when you make your choices.

Sincerely,

In the first example, *I* and *me* are used 10 times, but the letter still makes it easy for Mrs. Jones to correct her mistake. In the second example, *you* and *your* are used 11 times. Yet the second letter—even though it says *you* repeatedly—blames the reader and actually implies that she will have to suffer the consequences of her mistake.

The "you" attitude means putting yourself in the reader's place. You feel for the reader, understand the reader's position, and genuinely attempt to look after his or her interests.

EXERCISE

Rewrite the following "I" attitude sentences so that they have a considerate "you" quality.

1. I wish to apply for the position of stenographer as advertised in yesterday's *Daily Gazette*.

---

2. I am particularly eager to join your company, Mr. Watkins, because I know of its reputation for promoting promising employees.

---

3. Our company wishes to announce our Grand Opening.

4. We wish to call attention to the fact that we are in the sheet metal business in this city with a ten-year record of service. We are in a position to give good service, and we will be glad to give an estimate anytime.

5. In reply to inquiry of August 2, this is to say that Booklet No. 5 will not be reprinted for 60 days; and we regret, therefore, that we cannot send a copy at this time.

6. We cannot quote you a price until we have seen the specifications.

Say It Simply

Another important consideration is to say just enough, and to say it as simply as possible. This means omitting repetitious, outmoded words and phrases, which contribute to making messages long and pompous, and replacing fad words and jargon. In theme writing, fad words and jargon may help to create a special effect, but they are undesirable in business correspondence.

Remember to say just enough to achieve the purpose of your message. When you have done this, you have attained unity and organization. Avoid the jargon of the "grand" or the antiquated styles of business writing. Here is a "Jargoneer's Checklist," a guide for apprentice jargoneers who wish to make their writing longer, duller, and more complicated:

1. Since original thoughts are hard to think of, use a cliché whenever possible.
2. Always substitute an archaic, pompous word for an up-to-date conversational word.
3. Use the general word instead of the specific. This keeps the reader awake, guessing at your vague meaning.
4. If you can think of a long, complicated word to take the place of a short, simple word, use the inflated word.
5. Make all active sentences passive.
6. Choose one type of sentence construction and never vary from it. This gives your letters a dull, monotonous tone, which has a certain dignity.

Are you a jargoneer? Take a look at some of the following outmoded words and phrases, unnecessary repetitions, and overworked words and phrases that the true jargoneer never misses a chance to use.

Outmoded Words and Phrases

OUTMODED	SUGGESTED SUBSTITUTIONS
At an early date	**Soon (or give exact date)**
At that time	**Then**
At this time, at the present time, at the present writing	**Now, at present**
Due to the fact that	**As, because, since**
Enclosed please find	**Enclosed is**
In the event that	**In case, if**
Recent date	**(Give exact date)**
The writer	**I, me**
Under separate cover	**By freight (or whatever means of sending)**
Up to this writing	**Previously**
Wish to acknowledge	**Your letter of July 10**
Your check in the amount of	**Your check for**

Unnecessary Repetitions

AVOID	USE	AVOID	USE
And etc.	Etc.	Final completion	Completion
At about	About	Lose out	Lose
Both alike	Alike	May perhaps	May
Check into	Check	Near to	Near
Complete monopoly	Monopoly	New beginner	Beginner
Continue on	Continue	Over with	Over
Cooperate together	Cooperate	Past experience	Experience
Customary practice	Practice	Rarely ever	Rarely
Depreciate in value	Depreciate	Refer back	Refer
During the course of	During	Same identical	Identical
Endorse on the back	Endorse	Up above	Above

Overworked Words and Phrases

OVERWORKED	SUGGESTED SUBSTITUTIONS
Along the lines of	Like
At all times	Always
By means of	By
In the near future	(State the approximate or exact time)
Inasmuch as	Since
Awful	Terrifying
Bad	Inexcusable
Fabulous	Spectacular
Good	Choice
Lively	Delightful

Avoid Fad Words Like fads in clothing, certain words are popular for a while and are beaten to death with overuse. Avoid them. Examples of some words to avoid are given below along with suggestions for words that might be used in their place. Sometimes, however, it will be necessary to reword or rearrange the sentences in order to use the suggested words.

AVOID	USE	AVOID	USE
Profitwise	Profit rate	Corporate posture	Image
Finalized	Completed	Accountability	Answerable
Charismatic	Appealing or attractive	Sensitize	Feel

EXERCISES

1. Rewrite the following sentences, deleting irrelevant material and unnecessary repetitions, making the appropriate substitutions for any outmoded expressions and fad words, and including a feeling for the reader.

   a. We hereby acknowledge receipt of your order and assure you that said order will have the immediate attention of our staff.

   b. I would like to take the liberty of asking that you grant me an interview.

   c. We are pleased to advise that our prices are as low as those of any other candy jobber.

   d. We acknowledge receipt of your letter of the most recent date, with reference to the balance of your account in the amount of $750.

   e. We have cooperated together and started to commence the necessary processing required to establish the amount of your refund.

f. We wish to advise you that the subject amount will appear as a credit to you on your next rendered bill.

g. We have finalized arrangements to reestablish your service according to our practice regarding partial payment of unpaid bills.

h. The necessary requirements are that you make remittance by the last day of each month.

i. These two reports offer the same identical suggestions and recommendations.

j. He takes his customary walks all alone by himself every day.

2. The following bank letter does not convey a "you" attitude; uses useless words, unnecessary repetitions, and overworked phrases; and contains grammatical errors. Rewrite the message to make it more effective. Use another sheet of paper if necessary.

Dear Mr. Jacobs:

With reference to the discussion of certain securities of yours now in our possession. We should like to finalize this matter and get rid of this extra handling and shall clearly do so as soon as you make the first initial move. We have checked into this matter and written to you many times throughout the entire year making suggestions that certain securities be transferred from our name to your name, since you are the beneficiary under Mr. Smith's will. According to our records, from time to time dividend checks come to us in the mail because the securities remain under transfer from our name to your name. You should be fully cognizant of the fact that the stocks to which we make reference are the Silver Oil Company and Purchase Oil and Refinery Company. Due to this fact, and at the earliest possible date, we should appreciate it very, very much if you would bring in the above-mentioned securities, for the specific dividends paid on the stocks can be sent to you instead of being sent to us. A speedy reply from you to us would be duly appreciated profitwise.

Sincerely,

6

Editing for a Positive Message

Develop the Appropriate Tone "It's not always *what* you say—it's *how* you say it," and in no other case will this be more true than in business letter writing. Yes, how you tone up your writing or "how you say it" expresses your personality and that of your company. Your friendly nature, your helpful manner, your radiant personality, and your courteous gestures must be reflected through the *positive* tone of your messages. Since we have already discussed the importance of the "you" attitude, we have laid the groundwork necessary for an understanding of how to develop the appropriate tone.

Once you have realized the importance of the "you" attitude and have mastered its use, your messages will be sincere, courteous, direct, and honest rather than sharp, blunt, overbearing, and pompous. Only when the reader's point of view is foremost in your mind and in your writing will your messages be pleasant, persuasive, and convincing.

Many of your business letters—sales letters, collection letters, and application letters, to mention a few—will be written to arouse interest or to move the reader to action. The tone of these letters must be especially persuasive, vivid, and convincing. Therefore, they must appeal to basic wants and emotions.

Illustrated below are examples of a letter written to arouse the reader's interest and a letter written to move the reader to action.

Dear TEEN MAIL Reader:

Why are so many young adults like you joining the swing to SUPER, the magazine for today's sophisticated teens?

It's simple—we know modern teens have a wide range of interests, and we try to keep you posted on all of them. But we don't tell you what to do. We just present the latest facts, the newest happenings . . . and let you make up your own mind!

SUPER is lively, colorful, exciting. And now, exclusively for Teen Mail readers, you can have it sent to you personally at HALF-PRICE.

See for yourself why the smart set is swinging over to SUPER. Get 18 big issues (a full year and a half) for only $3.75! Detach and mail the postpaid card today—we'll bill you later.

Sincerely,

Dear Mr. Fowler:

Your account shows a balance due of $52.45 for children's clothing purchased during January and February. It is now April, and you still have not paid for these purchases.

By paying in full now, Mr. Fowler, you will maintain the excellent credit rating that you now enjoy and you will help us to meet our commitments.

A stamped, addressed envelope is enclosed for your convenience in mailing us your check for $52.45.

Sincerely,

Notice the vivid tone of the words used in the sales letter—*young adults, swinging, sophisticated, lively, colorful, exciting, smart set*. Note, too, how the sales letter has built an emotional appeal to teenagers based on their desire for identity with the "swinging set." Notice how the persuasive words of the collection letter—*maintain the excellent credit rating that you now enjoy, help us to meet our commitments*—have also built an appeal, a psychological appeal to Mr. Fowler to maintain his good image and to be fair.

Accent the Positive

One of the best ways to tone up your letters is to accent the positive or pleasant features and to eliminate the negative or unpleasant features. Consider your friend Bill: Bill is a pessimist—a real crybaby. Everybody is against him. Nothing ever goes right for him. Then consider your friend Charlie: Charlie is an optimist. He is cheerful, positive, and happy to be alive. Whom do you prefer to be with, Bill or Charlie?

Your readers will be critical of the letters they receive. They will avoid those letters that are pessimistic, negative, and unpleasant but will seek out those that are optimistic, positive, and pleasant. Positive language stresses the light rather than the dark side. Positive language emphasizes what can be done and leaves what cannot be done to implication.

Observe how the following pessimistic or negative sentences reveal an unpleasant tone. Then notice how the tone is improved in the optimistic or positive comparisons.

NEGATIVE	POSITIVE
We are sorry, but we cannot extend more than $200 worth of credit to you.	**You can buy up to $200 worth of merchandise on credit.**
You failed to state what size you wanted; therefore, we cannot send you the shoes.	**You will receive your Scarpa shoes within three days if you send us your shoe size on the enclosed card today.**
We cannot allow you to exchange this garment because it has been worn.	**If this garment had been returned before you wore it, we would have gladly exchanged it for you.**
We cannot deliver on Saturdays.	**Deliveries are made Monday through Friday only.**

The tone of *sorry, failed,* and *cannot* is negative and unpleasant. Notice how the first sentence becomes positive, and adopts a "you" attitude, when it is changed from *we cannot* to *you can*. In the second and third sentences, conditional words like *if* and *would* are used to transform a negative message into a positive message. And the last sentence is negative with an active verb but is positive with a passive verb!

Goodwill is an intangible quality that is extremely important to the success of a business. In order to have the goodwill of others, you must, of course, show goodwill in all your dealings. Businesses thrive on the

concept that "the customer is always right." And you, as a writer, must—even under the most negative circumstances—convey in your messages that "the reader is always right." Isn't this once again considering the situation from the reader's point of view?

EXERCISES

1. Rewrite the following negative sentences.

a. We cannot refund your $15.20 because you did not return the article within ten days of purchase.

---

b. We do not grant credit to people under eighteen years of age.

---

c. We are sorry to say that we cannot mail you 75 copies of *New Horizons.*

---

d. We regret that your order arrived in unsatisfactory condition.

e. We do not sell opaque stockings.

f. You failed to make a formal application for credit.

g. Your account of $7.50 is past due.

h. You cannot afford to destroy your credit rating.

2. Rewrite the following letter to improve the tone by stressing the positive aspects of a negative situation.

Dear Mrs. Carson:

You must have been disappointed and angry to have the raisins in your cake mix sink to the bottom. We deeply regret this unfortunate occurrence. It is no wonder that you were angry, and we apologize.

The only way raisins will not sink to the bottom in these cakes, however, is if they are chopped very finely. You won't be disappointed or angry anymore if you purchase our Streusel Coffee Cake Mix in which the raisins are finely chopped.

Once again, please accept our apologies for this unfortunate occurrence.

Cordially,

Check Your Spelling and Grammar

Another *must* when editing your message is to be sure that your spelling, grammar, punctuation, capitalization, and so on, are faultless. Refer to a dictionary or to a manual on English usage to check your spelling, word division, and grammar. See the Reference Section at the end of this book for a summary of the principles of punctuation, capitalization, number, and abbreviation style.

Review the Final Form

Some communications are very difficult to read simply because they are poorly arranged and poorly typed. If such is the case, the reader is distracted from the message. To make your messages readable, take special care that your letters and other communications make a good appearance. Which of the following letters do you feel is more likely to attract and hold the reader's attention—Example 1 or Example 2?

Example 1

The Everett Furniture Company
Raleigh Court, Greensboro, North Carolina 27411 (919) 555-2184

August 28, 19--

Mrs. Marion Baer
119 Hunter Avenue
Fan wood, New Jersey 07023

Dear Mrs. Baer:

Thank you for telling us that the table which we sent you last week was damaged when you received it. Of course, none of us wants to sel l a product that does notmeet our high standards.

The wood for the oak table that you bought was imported and was selected with care by our experts. The top piece was chosen for its fine grain and was rubbed by hand with a special polish that not only will bring out the natural beauty of the grain but also will protect the wood and preserve it for many years to come. Needless to say,,we do not want so fine a piece of furniture to be marred in any way, so we shall send one of our expert woodworkers to repair your beautiful dining room table.

Within the next weekor so, our service center will call to arrange an appointment with you. We know that when our expert repairs your table , it will be in perfect condition.

Sincerely,

Frances A. Sellers

Frances A. Sellers
Director of Customer Relations

FAS eh

Example 2

The Everett Furniture Company
Raleigh Court, Greensboro, North Carolina 27411 (919) 555-2184

August 28, 19--

Mrs. Marion Baer
119 Hunter Avenue
Fanwood, New Jersey 07023

Dear Mrs. Baer:

Thank you for telling us that the table which we sent you last week was damaged when you received it. Of course, none of us wants to sell a product that does not meet our high standards.

The wood for the oak table that you bought was imported and was selected with care by our experts. The top piece was chosen for its fine grain and was rubbed by hand with a special polish that not only will bring out the natural beauty of the grain but also will protect the wood and preserve it for many years to come. Needless to say, we do not want so fine a piece of furniture to be marred in any way, so we shall send one of our expert woodworkers to repair your beautiful dining room table.

Within the next week or so, our service center will call to arrange an appointment with you. We know that when our expert repairs your table, it will be in perfect condition.

Sincerely,

Frances A. Sellers

Frances A. Sellers
Director of Customer Relations

FAS/eh

Another important consideration is the stationery that you use. Almost every company provides high quality, costly letterhead and memo stationery. Since this letterhead is usually professionally designed and printed to portray a good company image, you should take special care not to waste it. Also, don't use letterhead for second sheets! The second sheet should, however, match the quality and color of the letterhead stock.

Unless your employer wishes to have you follow the company's office manual for style, you may refer to any good reference book for typists or writers for suggestions on style and arrangement. For some of the most popular arrangement styles of business letters, see the end of the Reference Section of this book. Some employers require their workers to refer to the existing files for letter and memo styles and formats. In many cases you may find that these examples are different from those you have learned to follow in your training program. Be tactful if you offer recommendations for modernizing the company's correspondence. Your employer has the right to dictate which styles you are to use.

7

Writing Requests and Thank You's

As an office worker, you will often write routine request letters and memos. Although these requests are not difficult to write, you should remember that they, too, must be well written if they are to achieve their purpose.

Everyday Requests

In writing a routine request letter, your most important responsibility will be to include all the information the reader will need to fill your request. It is always wise to keep your request as brief as possible, but not at the expense of being brusque or omitting important details. An incomplete request forces your reader to write you for more information. And if your reader must write to you to ask for more details, you have violated a rule of courtesy.

Remember the "you" attitude. If you consider the situation from the reader's point of view, you will include all the necessary information. Sometimes it will even be to your advantage to enclose a stamped, addressed envelope so that your reader can meet your request more easily. Of course, it is always essential to include your return address on the letter itself. Yet this rule of courtesy is often violated, especially when the request is of a personal nature and a letterhead is not used. Are you being considerate when you force your reader to file your envelope because your letter does not contain a return address?

Requests for Materials. When making a request, be sure you have a clear mental picture of what you want, and be sure you convey this same clear picture to your reader. If possible, address your request for materials to a particular individual. Sometimes, doing so may require extra effort on your part, such as a local telephone call to the company. If it is impractical to obtain the individual's name, write to the specific department that will handle your request. For example, if you are asking a particular firm for a description of its employee benefits, you should address your request to the personnel department; if you are asking for advertising literature, you should address it to the advertising department; and so on.

A letter requesting free materials is usually brief and easy to write. Obviously, you are in a position to get what you ask for, and the reader is eager to send it to you. It will not be necessary to make a strong plea. However, even though such letters are easy to write, good writers use their best writing style for every letter because they are continually striving to improve their writing ability. Writers become good at their craft only by doing lots and lots of writing.

Even for routine request letters, good writers always maintain a courteous "you" attitude. For example, it is courteous and shows good common sense to indicate how you intend to reimburse your reader for any mailing costs involved, and it is presumptuous to request several copies without assuming some cost for mailing. If only one copy of a pamphlet or other item is requested, a stamped, addressed envelope may sufficiently cover the mailing cost.

Look at the following example of a request for free literature:

> **Will you please send us a copy of your free pamphlet, Ahead of the Game, published in June, 19—. Every advertising firm on the West Coast has been singing the praises of your advertising brochure.**
>
> **Since our marketing forum will be held from March 15 to 16, we would appreciate receiving the pamphlet by March 10.**
>
> **A stamped, addressed envelope is enclosed.**

Notice that this letter contains all the information that the reader will need to respond favorably to the request. It includes dates—always a good idea—so that the reader is aware of the time requirements. And the enclosed envelope makes it easy for the reader to respond.

The writer of this letter should be commended for not making the usual beginner's mistake of thanking the reader in advance. It is presumptuous for a writer to use the same letter both to make a request and to thank the reader. Since the writer is asking for something, it seems only courteous to allow the reader the privilege of saying "yes" or "no." A message of gratitude should be extended only after the request has been granted.

EXERCISE

Assume you are employed by the Winthrop Publishing Company, 341 East Washington Street, Wheeling, West Virginia 26003. You are to write to the Meredith Paper Company, 2385 Baymiller Street, Hamilton, Ohio 45012, for 75 copies of their free instructional pamphlet, *New Selling Techniques,* used to train marketing persons in the latest sales methods. You wish to have these pamphlets by January 9, in time for a sales conference from January 10 to 13.

Requests for Information. Letters requesting information vary depending upon how general or how specific the request is. In some cases you may not be exactly sure of what you want or of what the reader has that you can use. What you are doing, in effect, is asking the reader to come up with some suggestions that will help you.

In such situations, you must state your problem specifically. And be reasonable. Don't ask for the moon and expect to get it! Note the following example: "I am interested in teaching. Will you send me all the information you have about teaching." Such requests for "all there is to know" about computers, selling techniques, and so on, are unreasonable and probably will not be filled.

Read the following excerpt from a request made to a postage meter company:

> **To handle our monthly volume of letters more efficiently, we should like to buy or rent a postage meter machine. Since we now mail approximately 500 letters a month, we are interested in your P-36 model.**
>
> **Will you please answer the following questions on your P-36 model machine:**

1. **Do you sell this machine? If so, what is its complete selling price?**
2. **Do you rent this machine? If so, what is the monthly rental cost?**
3. **Does this machine print an advertisement?**
4. **Does this machine seal envelopes?**

This example is effective because it is specific. Notice how the writer itemized each question, making it easier for the reader to understand the request. Also notice that the questions asked are brief and within reason and that they allow the reader to organize the answers. Instead of including the trite expression "We shall appreciate your reply as soon as possible," the writer assumed that the reader would give this request prompt attention. Obviously, the writer had no deadline; otherwise, he or she would have asked for the information by a definite time.

EXERCISE

You plan to enroll at the University of South Florida this fall but are unsure of what procedure to follow. Write a letter to the University of South Florida, Tampa, Florida 33620, requesting information about admissions procedures.

Request Memos. Requests made within a business firm are typed on memo forms. Sometimes a request from one employee to another is made orally; however, if the request requires the spending of money or is complex, it should be stated in writing, even if it has been discussed beforehand. The request should be stated in writing so that the specific details of the request—and any reply to it—are on file for the record. The request should also be in writing so that the person to whom you are writing can get further approval if necessary. Consider the following memo:

TO:	**L. Joe Cotton**	**FROM:**	**Betty Shuster**
SUBJECT:	**Accounting Seminar**	**DATE:**	**May 13, 19—**

The attached brochure describes the 23d Annual Accounting Seminar to be held in Birmingham, Alabama, from July 14 to 20. It looks like a good program, and I would like to attend.

Notice the sessions on developing five-year plans for comptrollers. As you are aware, I will be faced with this job shortly, and I can certainly use any information I can get to improve my Management-by-Objectives program. I estimate my expenses will be about $250, including air transportation. My assistant, David Bringall, will be able to handle my responsibilities while I am away.

The writer has given her supervisor enough information so that if necessary he can take it to his superior. By including the brochure, she has given Mr. Cotton an opportunity to evaluate the reasonableness of her request. The tone is convincing and is appropriate for writing to a supervisor who may have to ask for further approval.

EXERCISE

Write a memo to your supervisor (use your teacher's name) requesting permission to take two extra days off in June (the 7th and 8th—Thursday and Friday) to attend the wedding of your cousin who lives in Boston, Massachusetts. You are to be in the bridal party, and you have some last-minute things to do, including attending the wedding rehearsal. You have a long trip to Boston ahead of you.

TO:	**FROM:**
SUBJECT:	**DATE:**

(Continued on page 58.)

Requests for Reservations. Most people make hotel reservations by telephone, especially for those hotels which have toll-free telephone numbers. It is not unwise, however, to write a letter requesting a hotel reservation. The letter provides a record for you and encourages the hotel to mail you a written confirmation. In any event, when either telephoning or writing for such a reservation, you should request a written confirmation. If you have ever gone to a hotel and found that there was no record of your reservation, you will appreciate the importance of getting a written confirmation!

When writing for reservations, be sure to include the exact arrival date and any late afternoon or evening arrival information. If you are a member of a group attending a convention, be sure to mention that fact in your letter because you may be entitled to a special rate.

Consider the following hotel reservation request:

> **Will you please reserve a single room with shower for Mr. Dan Wheeler for Friday, October 16. Because of a late flight, Mr. Wheeler will check in around 10 p.m.**
>
> **Mr. Wheeler will be attending the Data Processing Workshop at your hotel on October 17 and will check out on that morning.**
>
> **Please confirm this reservation before October 5.**

The hotel reservation clerk will quickly read and understand this message. If a room is available, Mr. Wheeler will get it.

EXERCISE

You are employed by Mr. John Freeman, vice president of Cranston Laboratories, 1214 East Aquila Street, Hartford, Connecticut 06118. He has asked you to write to the Sitwell Inn, 3578 Highway 44, Lewiston, Maine 04240, to reserve a single room for the nights of March 3 and 4. He prefers a shower and a double bed. He is familiar with the rates and checkout times at the Sitwell, since he always stays there when in Lewiston.

____

____

____

____

____

____

____

____

Requests for Appointments. Many business executives frown upon people who just drop in on them, and they may refuse to see such visitors. Therefore, it is wise to request an appointment, either by telephone or in writing, instead of arriving unexpectedly.

Letters requesting appointments should be very courteous. Remember these are not demands, they are requests. Consider the following example:

Dear Mrs. Ruiz:

I plan to be in New York for three weeks in July. I would love to see your word processing center in operation.

Sincerely,

Obviously, this letter is not specific enough to be accepted or refused. In fact, no request has been made. The real purpose of the trip is not clear, and the time of the visit is vague. It is presumptuous to think that Mrs. Ruiz will spend three weeks in July waiting for this visitor. Notice the tactless and demanding tone of the letter.

EXERCISE

How would you revise the request for an appointment with Mrs. Ruiz?

Special Requests

You've been working for several months now, and each day your employer, Mr. Chin, is showing more confidence in your letter-writing ability. Today he stopped at your desk and said,"It looks as if our office-supplies sales representative has forgotten about us, and I don't have a catalog or price list. You had better write the company and order enough paper, envelopes, and return cards for the special mailing planned for next month. Remember, we don't have much time, so let's handle this letter with special care."

This is considered a special order because it requires a letter that you will not have to write often. Usually, you place your orders directly through your sales representative, using carefully planned and constructed order blanks and requisition forms. These are nearly foolproof and should be used whenever possible; however, many goods and services are ordered by letter.

EXERCISE

In the space below, write to the Gopher Paper Company to order white bond paper (8½ by 11 inches), envelopes (No. 10), and return cards (3½- by 8½-inch card stock) needed for a direct-mail campaign of 5,000 pieces. Your representative's name is Myrna Greco.

Analyze the following order letter; then compare it with your similar order letter to the Gopher Paper Company.

Mr. Sidney Gertz
Grand Typewriter Sales
140 Second Avenue South
Hopkins, MN 55343

Dear Mr. Gertz:

Please rush the following items as listed in your new June catalog by parcel post by January 10.

2 doz. Typewriter ribbons, black nylon, for Standard Grand, @ $1	**$24.00**
1 doz. Typewriter ribbons, black carbon, for Electric Grand, @ $2	**24.00**
1 box Typewriter erasers, Stik-a-Pen, brush end, light green, @ $.33	**8.25**
TOTAL	**$56.25**

You may bill the items and delivery charges to our regular monthly charge account.

Sincerely,

This special order letter illustrates a good form, one that is attractive, clear, and complete. Displaying each item requires more space but ensures that the reader will understand all the details.

Was your special order letter to the Gopher Paper Company as attractive, as clear, and as complete? Use the following checklist to evaluate your letter to Gopher and all other order letters that you may write.

1. Was your order complete? Was what you wanted crystal clear? Check your letter for the following:

a. Did you open with a definite request, such as "Please ship the following," or did you hint at what you wanted, as in "I should like to have"?

b. Did you include a description of the goods wanted? (Remember, you did not have a catalog or a price list when you wrote to the Gopher Paper Company.) Did you describe the goods completely and in a logical order, such as:

Quantity
Units (pounds, bushels, gross, dozens)
Catalog number (when you are ordering from a catalog)
General description (brand or trade name)
Specific details (color, style, size, weight)
Unit and total price

c. Did you carefully state shipping instructions?

If you had no special preference, did you specifically state "Ship the best way possible"?
If you had a preference, did you name the specific carrier and route?
If you needed the goods in a hurry, did you give a specific deadline?

d. Did you remember to include terms of payment and type of remittance?

If payment on delivery is the method customarily used, did you refer to it?
If you included the remittance, did you refer to the enclosed check?

If you wanted the amount added to your established account, did you indicate this?

2. Did you arrange and tabulate your letter so that the person handling the order can identify the items quickly and not overlook any?

    a. Did you set up a table?
    b. Did you single-space the description of each item?
    c. Did you double-space between items?
    d. Did you use abbreviations and symbols in describing the items?
    e. Did you capitalize the first letter of each description?
    f. Did you use leader lines to connect the items to prices?

3. Did you maintain a friendly, courteous tone? Were you as concise as possible?

EXERCISES

1. Write a letter to order four different items of your choice from a large mail-order house or department store. The items might be a pair of house slippers, two shirts or blouses, a belt, and a hat. You have a catalog in this instance, but no order blank. Be sure to include all the information the reader will need in order to select the goods from a large stock, ship them according to your wishes, and bill you for them (you do not have a charge account). Remember that mail-order houses must collect shipping expenses and state sales taxes, if applicable.

(Continued on page 64.)

2. Write a letter to a successful, highly paid secretary in your area requesting help in initiating a program of salary reviews for the secretaries in your firm.

Thank You's

All of us realize the importance of saying "Thank you" in oral communications; it is no less important in written communications. When you have received a helpful reply to your letter of request, you are correct in writing a letter of appreciation to thank your correspondent. If you are ever in doubt about whether to write a letter of thanks, write it. What can you lose? Simply say "Thank you," and don't preface it with "*I want to* thank you." *Thank you* is the most "you" attitude phrase you can use. Why preface it with *I want to* and weaken the forcefulness of the statement?

Ending a letter with the trite and stereotyped "Thanks again" also weakens the effectiveness of the letter. It is redundant, since you have already stated this in your first sentence. If you can honestly and sincerely state how the reply has helped you, do so and end your letter.

Consider the following thank-you letter:

> **Thank you for your informative and well-illustrated brochure, Getting Ahead of the Pack.**
>
> **All the sales representatives in our regional office are eager to put your ideas to work.**

This letter is brief, courteous, and sincere in tone. It is an effective thank you.

EXERCISES

1. You wrote a letter to Carl Johanson, promotion manager for the Boston Red Sox, asking for an autographed team picture for your nephew's birthday. You received a prompt reply, and your nephew was delighted with the picture. Write an appropriate letter of thanks.

2. You wrote to Midwestern Mills, Minneapolis, Minnesota 55443, and asked for information about their schedule of Future-Homes Tours. They informed you that they have tours at 10:15 a.m. and 2:15 p.m. on Tuesdays and Thursdays and accommodate small or large groups. Write a letter thanking them for this information even though you will be unable to take advantage of the tours.

8

Answering Request Letters

As a business worker, you will be answering request letters as well as writing them. Such responses to requests, like all other types of business correspondence, should help to create goodwill. The "yes" letter—one that grants the writer's request—is the easiest to write. After a brief "thank you" for the request, a positive statement is made giving the information, answering the questions, or indicating that certain materials will be mailed to the reader. However, not all replies can say "yes" as we shall see later in this chapter.

Answering Everyday Requests

The most important rule to follow in answering requests is to write the replies *promptly*. Every reply should be courteous, brief, and specific. If a request is made in the form of paragraphs, answer in the form of paragraphs. If the request is made in the form of enumerations, answer in the form of enumerations. Consider, for example, the following response to the letter of request on pages 55 and 56:

Thank you for your interest in the Randolph Speedy Mailers. You will enjoy reading the enclosed brochure, which describes our P-36 model in detail.

It is to your advantage to purchase the P-36 Speedy Mailer on a rental-purchase plan. This plan allows you to make rental payments with an option to buy.

As indicated in the enclosed brochure, businesses with a monthly volume of 500 letters "sing the praises" of the Randolph Speedy Mailers.

You will be pleased to know that the P-36 Speedy Mailer prints advertisements and stamps the envelopes in one simple operation (see page 8). It also seals the envelopes with ease and speed (see page 9).

This letter is specific, and the paragraphs make it relatively easy for the reader to follow and respond to the message.

Now consider this response:

Thank you for your interest in the Randolph Speedy Mailers. You will enjoy reading the enclosed brochure, which describes our P-36 model and answers your questions in detail.

1. **You may buy the P-36 Speedy Mailer, but it is to your advantage to rent this machine with an option to buy.**
2. **The rental charge is only $15 a month. The cost of the meter is, of course, proportionate to the amount of postage used (see page 8).**
3. **The P-36 Speedy Mailer prints small advertisements as it meters envelopes—all in one simple operation (see pages 8–9).**
4. **The P-36 Speedy Mailer also seals each envelope automatically.**

If you have more questions—or if you'd like to see a demonstration of the Speedy Mailer in operation—please call our representative in your area, Connie Wiener, at 555-1234. She will be happy to make an appointment at your convenience.

This letter is more specific than the previous example and makes it easier for the reader to respond because it uses more concise enumerations.

Consider yet another response to a request letter:

Thank you for your kind remarks concerning my newest publication, Human Relations at Work.

A complimentary copy was mailed to you on March 3. After you have had an opportunity to review this book in more detail, please write to me and let me know what you think of it for classroom use.

This letter has a courteous tone that compliments the reader by implying that the reader's comments will be valued by the author.

EXERCISES

1. Respond to a request for literature:

You are employed by the Meredith Paper Company, 2385 Baymiller Street, Hamilton, Ohio 45012. Mr. Jacob Levy, sales manager of the Winthrop Publishing Company, 341 East Washington Street, Wheeling, West Virginia 26003, has requested 75 copies of your instructional pamphlet *New Selling Techniques.* He needs these copies by January 9. You have had excellent reviews of this pamphlet by other business firms. You find, however, that you can spare only 15 copies now, for the supply is running low and will not be replenished until after January 9. Write a letter of response to Mr. Levy.

2. Acknowledge a request for information:

As secretary to the head of the Personnel Department at Lacey's Department Store, New York, you receive a request from Miss Janet Thorne, a student at New York State University, asking for information about the fringe benefits your company provides for its employees. She is writing a research paper for her marketing course and needs the information by the week of November 13. She specifically asks for information on medical insurance, stock options, and pension plans. You have a circular, *Lacey's and You*, which explains your benefits program. Answer her letter.

Answering Special Requests

Filling a Complete Request. Just as special order letters must be written with extra care, so must replies to these special orders be handled with extra care. Probably the most commonly written reply will be one which acknowledges an order and tells the reader that the goods or services are on their way. This type of letter has one major goal—to build goodwill. Like the letter granting a favor, it is positive and is pleasant to write. (As you will see later in this chapter, a reply letter that acknowledges an incomplete order or refuses a favor is, because of its negative message, more difficult to write.) Obviously, the best thing to do with a special order is to fill it immediately, or to at least inform the person when the order will be filled. Anytime there is a delay, the reader should be informed. Writers who attempt to improve public relations in every letter they write are keen enough to realize that the letter acknowledging an order can promote goodwill. As already stated, the letter that tells the buyer "All right—your order is on its way" is positive and easy to write. However, it must accomplish certain things.

If the primary objective of a letter is to create goodwill, it will be the writer's goal to emphasize the things that will have high reader interest. For example, if the shipment can be made exactly to the customer's specifications, this news alone will be good news and should be told immediately and with enthusiasm. Less important things such as when the order was received, details of packing, and payment arrangements should be included, but they should be placed in subordinate positions.

EXERCISE

Consider the following three examples:

1. We were pleased to receive your order, and it will be shipped today.
2. Your order was shipped today, and you should receive it soon.
3. Your Order 236 should arrive on Tuesday, June 25, as we shipped it airmail today.

Which of these three opening sentences do you consider the most reader-oriented? Why?

If you selected the third example, you have considered the reader. You have given specific information so that the reader is not left worrying and wondering when the order will arrive. It is positive and will be accepted as good news.

Expressing Appreciation. Once you have enthusiastically given the good news, you may then proceed to discuss the other details—practical aspects such as when the order was received, packing and payment arrangements, and so on. Perhaps the following example will clarify this discussion:

> **Your order for 20 cases of assorted Rosedale Farm Vegetables should reach you on Monday, as we shipped it by truck yesterday. You will be pleased to know that our Invoice 264 totaling $170.10, including delivery charges of $17.50, was charged to your regular charge account No. 411425, as you requested in your order of April 6.**

Do you see how this message gets off to a good start and still brings in the practical details? You may notice that the writer has not said thank you, even though this is an excellent opportunity to show appreciation for the order. Although the reader is more interested in the good news of positive action, you should by all means show your appreciation in the letter—but show it after you have indicated action. Be careful, of course, to avoid trite expressions such as "Much obliged for your order" or "Welcome to our family of charge customers." Sometimes the tone of your letter will be the only thing necessary to indicate your appreciation.

EXERCISE

Using the following example for your opening paragraph, complete the letter. Follow these suggestions: Show appreciation without being gushy, welcome your new customer, resell your product, and end your letter with a friendly comment that will build goodwill.

> **Your order for 20 cases of assorted Rosedale Farm Vegetables should reach you on Monday, as we shipped it by truck yesterday. You will be pleased to know that our Invoice 264 totaling $170.10, including delivery charges of $17.50, was charged to your regular charge account No. 411425, as you requested in your order of April 6.**

____

____

____

____

____

____

____

____

Analyze your letter using the following checklist; write *Yes* or *No* next to each question. Be objective in your analysis!

_____ **a.** Is your letter direct and reader-oriented? Did it avoid wishy-washy idle chatter like "We received your order and were happy to fill it"?

_____ **b.** Did you include the practical details; for example, description of goods and method of payment?

_____ **c.** Did you attempt to sincerely develop goodwill by using a "you" attitude, thanking the writer for the order, welcoming a new customer, and closing with a friendly—but not trite—comment?

_____ **d.** Did you attempt to resell your product, and did you offer profit-making suggestions and sales promotion ideas?

If you answered "yes" to all the questions on the checklist, you can be sure that your letter will receive an enthusiastic welcome and that you have handled this special order with care.

Asking for More Information. Acknowledging a complete and specific special order with positive action is much easier and more pleasant than acknowledging an incomplete order. When you receive an incomplete order, you may be annoyed by the inconvenience and the delay caused by the writer's oversight. This attitude, however, does not keep customers or increase company profits. Your objectives will be to minimize the unfortunate results of incomplete orders, to avoid embarrassing the writer, and to get the information needed to complete the order.

It is not necessary to trace the oversight step by step; in fact, it probably does not have to be stated at all, merely implied. Putting the reader on the spot is antagonizing. Just as indefensible is the apologetic manner of blaming yourself for not being able to understand the order. Both of these approaches question the reader's intelligence. Your primary concern should be to get the information necessary to complete the order. This is the only way to handle this negative situation.

Remember that any chatty opening, if you use such an approach, should be brief and sincere and should set the stage for the negative message. Avoid overusing negative words. One effective opening is to refer to the desirability of the product. The opening could also refer to the actual order and indicate appreciation for the order.

Consider the following example:

Dear Miss DiAngelo:

You will be pleased with the modern, clean, general appearance of your correspondence when you use the variety of typestyle elements available for your new Manning electric typewriter. Thank you for your October 15 c.o.d. parcel post order for four electric, nickle type elements.

So that you can get exactly the type style you wish, will you please review the enclosed catalog and make a selection. As you will notice, we have marked in red those styles which have been the most popular.

After reviewing the catalog, will you please check your selections on the enclosed stamped, addressed order card and mail it

to us today. Upon receipt of this card, we will mail your four electric type-style elements immediately, as all models are in stock.

Sincerely,

This letter does a good job because it does not criticize the customer for not providing sufficient information to fill her order. The opening paragraph restates the desirability of the product. The next paragraph invites the reader to make a selection. The final, friendly note makes it easy for the reader to reply and is positive and not stereotyped like "A speedy reply would be greatly appreciated."

EXERCISE

David Hoitsma, manager of the Advertising Department of your company, recently attended a meeting in Chicago. In response to your request for a statement of his expenses, he sent you a memo simply stating the total amount. He neglected to include an itemized statement of his expenses, as well as receipts for his transportation, hotel bills, and any entertainment expenses over $25.

As secretary to the general manager, write the necessary memo to Mr. Hoitsma.

TO: **FROM:**
SUBJECT: **DATE:**

Now check to make sure you did not include any of the following expressions in your memo to Mr. Hoitsma:

1. "I find that you did not include," or "I regret that I cannot complete." (Negative expressions and words should be completely avoided.)
2. "Thank you for your memo." (Stereotyped, cold expressions should be avoided.)
3. "A reply is needed as soon as possible." (Too shopworn; be more specific.)
4. "Tell me how you spent the money so I can process your expense report." (Lacks the tone of goodwill because it is demanding.)

Refusing a Request

Not all replies can say "yes" or merely ask for more information. Some replies must refuse readers' requests. Like the letter asking for more information, the letter or memo that says "no" to a request is negative in nature—more negative than an acknowledgment of an incomplete request. Therefore, refusals are difficult to write. However, even when you cannot supply all the answers or all the data requested, you can always offer some help or make some positive suggestion to maintain the reader's goodwill. Remember that every piece of correspondence must be courteous and should help create goodwill; but this is especially true of refusals.

Successful refusals begin on a positive note—never on a negative note! The reasons for the refusal should be developed logically so that the reader will understand that the refusal was not made on mere whim. And the refusal itself should be stated in a positive manner.

EXERCISE

The staff of *Hi-Lite* (a school newspaper) is attempting to pay part of its publication costs by selling leather and ceramic handicraft made by the students. The secretary of the staff has written a letter to your employer, who is the vice president of the Towers Department Store at the Tremont Plaza Shopping Center, requesting one of the store windows to display these goods from April 1 to 14. Towers Department Store has a company policy that only store merchandise can be displayed in its windows, and your employer lacks authority to change company policy.

Write a reply for your employer. Your employer takes great pride in the schools in the community and in no way wants to reflect a sorehead, unenthusiastic attitude. However, the request *cannot* be granted.

An analysis of your answers to the following questions will help you judge the effectiveness of your communication.

1. Did you begin your letter with a stereotyped, obvious beginning such as "Your letter of March 4 has been referred to me for a reply"?
2. Did you convey a negative tone? Did you avoid giving reasons for the refusal?
3. Did you present your reasons at a time in the letter when they were unimportant because the reader was already dejected by the brusque refusal? For example, did you say something like "Many requests are made for the use of our windows for display, and unfortunately all requests cannot be met. Therefore, to avoid any partiality, we must refuse all who ask"?
4. Did you hide behind company policy as in "Due to company policy, we will be unable to allow you to display your handicraft in our windows"?

5. Did you then remind your reader of the disappointment by adding "We hope that you will understand our reasons for refusing our display windows for your leather and ceramic handicraft"?
6. Did you end your letter with a trite "If we can be of any assistance in the future, please contact us"?

If you fell prey to any of the preceding pitfalls, remember that it is sometimes difficult to be tactful and considerate while saying "no." Here are some suggestions that beginners have found helpful in sincerely communicating their consideration for their readers. These suggestions should be applied only in situations where the reader and the writer are not personally acquainted. Once writers have polished their craft, they seldom need step-by-step suggestions such as these:

1. Begin with a neutral or positive beginning, such as "The *Hi-Lite* staff should be commended for developing ingenious ideas to raise money to finance their outstanding school newspaper."
2. Develop the reasons for not granting the request before actually refusing it, so that the refusal can be more easily accepted. For example, "Last year, Towers Department Store received more than 100 requests for use of their display windows by charities, high schools, colleges, church groups, and civic organizations. Which of the requests were to have priority? When would we be able to display our own store merchandise? These were some of the problems with which we were faced."
3. Refuse in the most positive manner possible, such as "For this reason, the management of the Towers Department Store has decided that display windows will be used to display store merchandise only, so that customers can always depend on Towers to display the latest in fashions."
4. Include an alternative, if possible. For example, "Because we enjoy reading your high-caliber school newspaper as much as the students do, may I suggest that you have your business manager call me at 555-6251 to discuss advertising space in your next issue. You can depend on us to advertise only things of student interest."
5. End on a pleasant note, such as "Best wishes for another good newspaper publishing year. Perhaps you may want me to talk to some of my business associates about advertising in the *Hi-Lite*."

9

Promoting Goodwill

Just as every business letter should be a sales letter, every business letter should also be a goodwill letter—a plain "being nice" letter. But if a letter's *primary* purpose is just to be nice or to promote goodwill, the letter is then categorized strictly as a goodwill letter—a letter to improve relations with the reader.

Goodwill letters are usually announcements and invitations and letters of sympathy, appreciation, congratulations, or praise. Goodwill letters are reader-oriented; there is practically no emphasis on the writer. Because they require a very personal approach, composing these letters calls for a wide range of flexibility on the writer's part.

Goodwill letters are personal business letters, and they may be written on company stationery or on plain paper, depending on the situation. Letterhead, however, is not suitable for very personal letters. Remember, also, that company letterhead takes away some of your individuality.

Expressing Appreciation

One of the personal business letters you will write is the "special thanks" letter—a letter to show appreciation for something special that has been done for you. Regardless of whether you think your reader expects some expression of appreciation or not, you should never neglect this opportunity to be nice.

Time is especially important in writing a "special thanks" communication. Promptness usually indicates sincere appreciation. Although promptness is usually commendable, there are situations when delaying your response is desirable. Let us say, for example, that you receive a letter from a job applicant who is not qualified for the job. If you respond to this letter on the same day, the applicant will feel that you didn't give the application much thought. In this case, a few days' delay is the best alternative. In other cases, letters of appreciation or "special thanks" may have greater impact at certain times of the year. For example, special thanks to prompt-paying customers may be sent right after the New Year.

EXERCISE

Let's see if you can write a "special thanks" letter. Write a letter to your minister, priest, or rabbi showing appreciation for a letter of recommendation written on your behalf. Assume that you were seeking either employment or admission to a college or vocational school.

Did you remember to do one of the following:

1. Lead off with the main message and tell your reader exactly why you were expressing thanks?
2. Lead up to a thank-you message by arousing the reader's interest with an attention getter before covering all the facts?

Either of these openings could have been used to show appreciation, provided that you unified the entire message by relating everything to appreciation.

Did you remember to:

1. Discuss any pertinent facts or observations?
2. Follow up with an indication that you will return the favor in the future, tell others, or remember the deed?

A follow-up letter of appreciation will bring back to your reader the pleasant, good feeling of being appreciated. When you write a follow-up letter, avoid trite, stereotyped expressions such as "Your service is greatly appreciated." Cold, pompous affirmations of appreciation are worthless.

Now that you've had a chance to analyze your attempt at writing a thank-you letter, you should have no trouble writing a letter for the following exercise.

EXERCISE

As a result of your persuasive letters, three prominent business executives served as consultants to an advisory council on hiring handicapped workers. With their help, the Hire the Handicapped program has been highly successful in your community. Write a thank-you letter to one of these business executives.

(Continued on page 82.)

Congratulating a Superior

Letters of congratulations show thoughtfulness and good manners and are also considered goodwill letters.

These letters should be written:

1. **Promptly** (preferably the same day that the news is received).
2. **Enthusiastically** (perhaps the beginning should be exclamatory).
3. **Informally**, with a conversational style in the body of the letter and also in the salutation and complimentary closing (use first-name basis in the salutation, and avoid *yours* in the complimentary closing).
4. **Sincerely** (show sincere interest in the reader; avoid using "good luck," which may indicate to the reader that luck accomplished the feat).

Consider the following situation: For the past two years you have been an accountant for Consolidated Motors Company. You report directly to Elvera DeKooning, who was named comptroller of the company about six months ago. Although you do not know your boss personally as well as you would like, you enjoy working for her and hope to get to know her better through your common interest in civic matters. She is an active member of the Dover County Civic Club, which you recently joined. Since your first meeting with Ms. DeKooning, she has asked you to call her Elvera.

In last night's *Daily Advance*, you read the announcement of Elvera DeKooning's election to the presidency of the Dover County Civic Club at the last meeting, which you were unable to attend. To take this opportunity to establish a closer working relationship, you offer your congratulations in the following letter:

Dear Elvera:

I congratulate you on being elected president of the Dover County Civic Club and compliment the members of the club for their wisdom in choosing you.

As a new member of the club, I look forward to the coming year under your leadership.

Sincerely,

Let's analyze this letter:

1. The tone of the message seems appropriate to the situation in view of the relationship between the writer and the reader.
2. It has a sincere, warm quality. There are no fawning or flattering statements directed to the reader; therefore, the writer cannot be accused of apple-polishing.
3. Even though the writer will probably also congratulate Ms. DeKooning in person, the written message makes it possible for the reader to share it with others.
4. In view of the purpose and subject of the message, the writer addresses the reader on a first-name basis, just as the writer would in a face-to-face conversation.

EXERCISES

1. Analyze the following letter and be prepared to discuss its strong and weak points.

Another milestone has been passed in your development of the best youth organization in the state of California.

It is unreasonable to expect that my appreciation for your excellent and untiring job can be expressed by the mere writing of words on a sheet of paper. Satisfaction and appreciation for your accomplishments can only be in terms of the contribution to the development of the fine youth involved in the vocational clubs in our state.

It is to this end that I would express not only my own appreciation, but the thanks of all the youth whom you have inspired and provided leadership to during the Leadership Conference. May you have the same good luck next year!

2. Write a letter of congratulations and good wishes from your employer, the marketing director for AK Visual Aids, to the production manager, David Phillips, for his tenth year of service to the company.

Making Announcements Announcements that tell your friends and business associates about something that has happened or is going to happen are also goodwill letters. Such personal business messages may be brief; sometimes a single sentence suffices, such as "The Advisory Council of the Washington Business and Office Association will meet at the Seattle

Civic Center at 7:30 p.m. on Monday, January 26, to discuss community survey plans."

For a lengthy announcement, you may wish to make the announcement, follow with a discussion of reasons, and then end with suggested action. Remember that the actual announcement is the major purpose of the message. The following announcement is an example of a message from a newly elected executive director.

> **Thank you for the opportunity to act as Executive Director for the Illinois Chapter of the Distributive Clubs of America. Before the year is over, I hope to meet every member individually. All of us have a common goal—preparing youth for the distributive occupations.**
>
> **I am enthusiastic about this new position and eager to get the activities going for this year. With your help, we can make this the DCA's best year in Illinois.**
>
> **As your Executive Director, I plan to give this job all my attention and effort. However, it will be you and your ideas and suggestions that will be the indicators of our future success. Let's rally for a successful year!**

EXERCISES

1. The Oreck's store on Michigan Avenue in Chicago has just completed the construction of a new store at the River Road Shopping Center. Write a form letter from your employer, who is the vice president of Oreck's, to your customers to announce your expansion.

(Continued on page 86.)

2. Consider the following announcement; then, in the space provided, attempt to improve it.

We have just recently sold our business to the Payton Company of Dallas, Texas. The Payton Company of Texas will in the near future be serving you and needless to say we have told them about our many customers who have been so good to us in the past and they are excited.

We thank you for the many years that you have patronized Diamond, Inc., and we regret that we will no longer be serving you. Thanks for everything and also for the interest you have shown us in the past.

Some of you have been customers for many, many years and we appreciate very much your confidence. Yes, indeed, it is sad to leave a roster of 25,000 charge customers and many other cash customers.

Expressing Sympathy

The most difficult goodwill letters to write are those expressing sympathy for someone who has experienced a personal loss. In writing a condolence, you should try to bring some comfort to the reader and let him or her know that you are sincerely interested. Although the printed card or message is a popular way of conveying this expression of sympathy, a well-written message sometimes adds a personal touch.

Condolences require careful and serious thought. Letters of condolence should be written:

1. **Promptly** (preferably on the same day you receive the news).
2. **Simply** (refer to the event that has occurred; then follow with an expression of sympathy).
3. **Sincerely** (use a serious tone; and offer to be of assistance when it is appropriate).

Consider the following letters:

Dear Mr. Harrigan:

All of us here at General Electronics are grieved by the news of the death of your president, Jean Rousseau. Please accept our most sincere sympathy.

Mrs. Rousseau was a true leader and served as an example to all of us in the community. Her charitable work with the March of Dimes will long be remembered.

Yes, indeed, the memory of Jean Rousseau will continue to serve as an inspiration to the members of the community of Green Plains.

Sincerely,

Dear Tom:

Your co-workers at Daffin Corporation were sorry to learn of your wife's illness. Please accept the flowers we have sent as sincere wishes that she will make both a fast and a complete recovery.

All of us mean it when we say "Get well."

Sincerely,

Both letters are simple and short, and both express sincere sympathy. Although the first letter reminisces a little bit, it doesn't dwell on the sorrow; it is perfectly acceptable.

EXERCISES

1. You have just learned of the tragic death of Dr. Willa Crawford, one of your former teachers, as a result of a car accident. Dr. Crawford was one of your favorite teachers because she always seemed to have enough time to meet with you to discuss both personal and school problems. In fact, she was also the adviser of the yearbook, and the two of you worked closely together on this project. You think it would be appropriate at this time to write a letter to Dr. Crawford's husband, whom you have met through the yearbook staff meetings held at the Crawford home.

2. The rising Minnesota River has forced families in the Savage, Minnesota, area to vacate their homes until the waters subside. The Governor of Minnesota has asked the federal government for funds for this disaster area. Write an open letter of sympathy to Chadwick Sommers, mayor of Savage, for your employer, who is an adviser for the Future Farmers of America in the adjacent community of Chanhassen. Offer the services of his youth group to help with sandbagging.

10

Selling by Mail

Almost every business letter attempts to sell something. For this reason, many people say, "Every business letter is a sales letter." In this chapter, however, *sales* letters will mean only those letters specifically intended to sell the products or services of a company.

More than likely, you will not have to write many sales letters. However, learning to write these letters can be of value to you. The experience of writing sales letters will make other letter writing easier, particularly writing letters of special request.

Another sound reason for developing the ability to write sales letters is that you will have an invaluable advantage in being able to appraise and evaluate the attempts of others, not to mention the practical personal applications that you will learn.

You have already become acquainted with the requirements of a good request letter: it must make a clear, definite request; it must motivate the reader to act favorably to that request; and it must be easy for the reader to respond to the request. These are also the basic requirements of a good sales letter.

Get the Facts Deciding how to slant your sales appeal in a sales letter will involve careful research. Getting the facts will mean that you will become fully aware of *what* and *to whom* you are trying to sell. This is necessary if you are to have any success in marketing your product or service.

What you are trying to sell must be conveyed to the reader in descriptive terms, such as size, shape, color, and other physical qualities. It stands to reason that the more you know about what you are trying to sell, the easier it will be for you to direct your sales appeal. The description you give will allow your reader to form a mental picture of your product or service. Yes, the description is very important; however, the functional use of the product or service will be even more important. But one should supplement the other.

Where will you go to find information about *what* you are trying to sell? Here are some sources:

1. The product itself—physical characteristics, unique features, durability.
2. The resource materials that go into the product—variety used ("ebony wood," "stainless steel," and so on), source of supply ("imported African mahogany," for example).
3. The manner in which it is produced—special equipment used ("deep-oven baked"), skills required ("handcrafted leather"), sanitary measures ("sterile gauze").

Where will you go to find out *who* will buy your product or service? Most often you will attempt to buy or rent lists of names of prospective customers with common interests. You might use lists of college graduates, high school graduates, magazine subscribers, teachers, and so on. Once you have selected the mailing list, you will have to know the following things about your prospective customers:

1. Is the customer a retail buyer or a wholesale jobber (one who sells to others)?
2. What is the customer's background?
3. What are the customer's needs?
4. What are the customer's likes and dislikes?

Although in direct-mail advertising or selling the same letter is sent to all the prospective customers on the mailing list, every letter has to sound as though it were written especially for each reader. For this reason, research of the prospective customer is of great importance.

Have a Plan

Once you get the facts, your next step is to develop a plan—a plan that will include everything that is necessary to put you on the right path to developing a powerful, polished sales message. Remember, this plan should meet all the requirements of a good request letter and should include all the specifics that are necessary to the particular situation. As a beginning writer, you may wish to utilize the following three-step plan. It could produce results for you.

1. Command attention and stimulate interest.
2. Describe and explain the product or service so that the customer will want to buy and use it.
3. Motivate prompt, easy-to-take action.

Command Attention. The money and time spent on the direct-mail campaign will be wasted unless the prospect reads the message. Your strategy should start, therefore, with the envelope itself. You may want to consider the following ideas that have been used to entice the prospective customer to open the letter and read it:

1. Make your correspondence resemble first-class mail (it will probably be third-class mail) by using precanceled stamps, imitation stamps, or metered mail.
2. Avoid using a return address so that your customer will be curious to open the letter.
3. Use a tan-colored window envelope with the prospect's name showing to give the impression that the enclosed material is important.
4. Address the envelope in longhand to reduce the suggestion of mass mailings.

In general, however, mass mailings are difficult to camouflage, and some of the prospective customers may recognize the above ideas. To avoid being phony, it may be wise to print or type on the envelope an attention-getting device such as "Invitation enclosed" or "Free gift inside."

The letter, too, must command attention, of course. One way to command attention is to make the sales letter as individualized as possible, even though it may be a form letter that will be sent to many prospective customers who are on a common-interest mailing list. Usually it is impractical to use an inside address; therefore, you should attempt to attract attention with a headline and then follow with a general salutation to the group, such as "Dear Student" or "Dear Homemaker." Also, using the exact date will probably be unwise, but since a date should be included, you could omit the day and say "March, 19—," for example. The other parts of the sales letter are basically the same as for other types of business letters. For example, parts such as the complimentary closing, signature, and reference initials are used to retain the authentic look of personalized communications.

The sales letter must arouse the curiosity of your reader so that he or she will be interested enough to read the beginning of your message. Anytime you can make a reader ask "What is this?" you have accomplished this objective, because the only way the reader can find out is to read on. The following attention getters have been used successfully to attract readers enough to ask "Just what is this all about?"

1. An exciting, stirring, never-used-before statement in bold type or color.
2. A headline in bold type or color.
3. An illustration, such as a cartoon or a clever drawing.
4. A gadget, such as a shiny new penny or a check.

It is wise to remember that whatever you use as your attention getter, it should be positive, in good taste, and enticing. Again, the only purpose of the attention getter is to make the reader ask "What is this all about?"

You will realize now how complex preparing a sales campaign can be. You must coordinate the envelope, letter, return card, and so on, and present a total sales package, a package that will attract the reader's attention and stimulate the reader's interest.

Stimulate Interest. The best way to prepare a strong sales message that will stimulate the reader's interest is to appeal to basic wants, because *basic wants* are (1) quickly aroused, (2) vigorous and strong, and (3) practically universal. Here is a list of basic wants and the activators or *drives* that make people go after these wants:

BASIC WANTS	DRIVES
Food, drink, and shelter	**Enjoyment of appetizing, satisfying food and drink and of a home or apartment**
Comfort	**Comfortable clothes, furnishings, and surroundings**
Security—freedom from fear and danger	**Elimination of fearful, painful, dangerous things**
Superiority over others	**Victory in every race—keeping up with the Joneses**
Attraction to the opposite sex	**Companionship, love, and affection of the opposite sex**
Social approval	**Acceptance by friends and associates**
Welfare of loved ones	**Provision for the welfare of loved ones**
Longer life	**Enjoyment of life—the possibility of living longer**

There are wants other than basic wants. These wants are considered *secondary wants* and are learned or acquired. They develop as we grow older and become more experienced and conscious of our position in society. For selling some products and services, appeals to these secondary wants can be very effective. Secondary wants are not, however, stimulated as quickly as basic wants. A list of secondary wants is shown at the top of page 95, along with examples of sentences that can stimulate them.

SECONDARY WANTS	EXAMPLES
Bargains	**"Make $1 do the work of $4."**
Information	**"Comparison proves the new Cold Air is a great refrigerator to buy. Look at these features."**
Cleanliness	**"Before and after—see what a difference Tinsley Shampoo makes?"**
Efficiency	**"New Smooth Oil starts easier! Makes your engine run cleaner, perform better, last longer."**
Convenience	**"A new instant coffee that tastes as good as your favorite ground coffee!"**
Dependability, quality	**"You can always count on a Wilson Job-Rated Truck!"**
Economy, profit	**"Buy the economy size and save!" And "These tires give 33% more wear."**
Curiosity	**"Don't read this advertisement unless . . . "**

The appeal you choose will depend upon the results of your study of both your product or service and your prospective customers. Once you have chosen the appeal you will use, you will be able to develop your plan for a successful, strong sales message.

As you have seen, a successful sales letter must command attention and spark the reader's interest. However, something more is needed if you expect the spark to catch fire. You must *satisfy* the interest you have aroused. You must provide a bridge, a realistic connection, or you will offend your reader's intelligence.

Consider the following example:

> **Have you noticed the beautiful stone drywall decorated with flowering shrubs and geraniums in front of your neighbor's home down the street? Whether you know your neighbor or not, you may want to take a look to see how sturdy the wall is, as well as**

how the decorative and colorful setting compliments that two-story house.

Your home can have the same flair of natural charm in a distinctive setting that will compliment your home for less than $200.

This message is positive and in good taste. It uses an attention getter that sparks interest and is pertinent to what the writer is trying to sell. In the second paragraph the writer satisfies the interest that was originally aroused.

Avoid attention getters that have no relation to the subject of the letter, such as the following:

1. Completely unrelated openings—"Beware! Vicious dog! We don't know if you have a dog or not, but we are willing to deliver 26 baby spruce pine trees right to your door for the exceptionally low price of $1.50 each."
2. Negative statements—"Are you ready to blow your brains out every day because you are plagued by door-to-door sales representatives? Assuming that you are, we hope you will appreciate our selling Handi-Pak hairbrushes by mail."
3. Remarks insulting to a person's intelligence—"Have you heard that the early bird catches the worm?"
4. Lecture-sermon types of openings—"As a taxpayer, you should be vitally concerned with the expenditures of your city officials."
5. Kidding kinds of openings—"Now you don't want to see me out of a job, do you? Well, if I can't sell you a new Speedy Vacuum, I may be out of a job."

EXERCISE

Draft an attention-getting, interesting opening for a letter to the business executives in your community encouraging them to purchase advertising space in your yearbook. All space is one size only—2 inches by 2 inches—at a cost of $50.

Describe and Explain. Another principle to consider in planning an effective sales message is to describe and explain the product or service. You will, of course, have to cover its physical characteristics. To understand the value of your product or service, your reader must have a vivid mental picture of it. Your reader will not be able to appreciate the explanatory message that follows your description unless you have successfully conveyed this picture.

Remember, this description and the explanatory message will be the significant factors that will stimulate the reader to purchase the product or service. The description will have to tell what your product or service will do for the reader by suggesting that one or more of the reader's wants will be satisfied. In other words, a sales letter should carry the same reader-oriented message of all request letters.

Do not try to bluff your reader! Just as the hard sell of the insincere sales representative is quickly recognized, the hard sell of the insincere message, too, is easily detected. Your product or service has to live up to your promises. A deliberate effort on your part to substantiate your claims will register positively with your reader. Many devices have been used successfully, such as:

1. Laboratory tests
2. Testimonials
3. Endorsements
4. Free samples
5. Trial periods
6. Money-back guarantees

EXERCISE

From the opening that you developed in the previous exercise, write a follow-up description that will explain the benefits of buying advertising space in your yearbook. Use the space provided on page 98.

Motivate Action. An effective sales message must also motivate prompt, easy-to-take action. You must give your reader a reason to act at once, because the highest point of interest is when the letter is still in your reader's hands. You will probably have to induce the reader to take prompt action with special discounts, trial periods, free samples, and so on. All these things may be ineffective, however, unless they are offered "for a limited time only." The reader who does not act immediately will probably never act.

To help motivate your reader to prompt action, you may also offer payment plans, delayed billing, or other such helpful measures. Addressed, stamped envelopes are effective, as are convenient order forms. The easier you make it for the reader to answer, the more eager he or she will be to do so. If you expect a reader to answer by telephone, make sure the telephone number is obvious and that extension numbers are given for departments. If a personal visit is necessary, it is important to describe the location and to indicate the store hours, parking facilities, public transportation, and so on.

Consider the sales appeal in the letter that begins at the top of page 99.

Dear Friend:

The Fund for the Improvement of the Environment needs your help to "Keep America Beautiful." In the past, we have distributed free litter bags to emphasize the need to free our environment from litter. By using them you help remind our community that FIE is devoted to making America a cleaner place in which to live.

Now we must reevaluate our total budget because of the public demand for us to expand our community services. For this reason, we must discontinue the FIE tradition of distributing litter bags without charge.

Will you help us continue this worthwhile service by buying your litter bags and distributing them to your customers? You can buy them for as little as $4.70 for 100 bags.

Check the number you will need on the enclosed stamped business reply card, and return it to us today. Your support will help FIE to "Keep America Beautiful."

Sincerely,

The writer does a nice job in this fund-raising letter, which differs slightly from a sales letter in that it does not promise the prospects a product or service. It asks them to support a cause. Appeals such as fund-raising letters cannot offer readers the explanation, description, and prompt action of sales letters. In fact, these tactics would be in poor taste for such letters. This writer presents the message in a dignified manner and attempts to instill in the reader a feeling of wanting to get on the bandwagon and make a contribution.

EXERCISES

1. Wind up your letter selling advertising space in your yearbook to the business executives in your community. Be sure to motivate them to act!

(Continued on page 100.)

2. Assume you work at the Breezy Cape Lodge on Willow Lake outside Brainerd, Minnesota, as a secretary for the sales and promotion manager. The editor of the magazine *The Great Outdoors* has just sent your boss a list of names of fishing enthusiasts residing in the Minnesota area. These prospects are prominent professional business executives. It is now April 20, and your boss wants you to try out your newly acquired sales-letter-writing skills by writing a letter urging these outdoor lovers to spend their vacations at your lodge. Since your resort is so popular, for the past two years you have had waiting lists; therefore, reservations should be made by May 10.

   Some of the facts you might include in your letter are:

   a. You have excellent bass and northern pike fishing.
   b. You operate a charter plane service from Minneapolis to Willow Lake.
   c. You require a $25 deposit for every reservation.
   d. You have other facilities, such as boats, cabins, beaches, a nine-hole golf course, and a nightclub for dancing.

   Perhaps your sales letter should put particular emphasis on emotional appeals and descriptions. Obviously, the pleasure, satisfaction, relaxation, and joy that a vacationer at your lodge can enjoy will be appealing to today's busy executive.

   Use the following space to write your sales-appeal letter. Describe any nonverbal techniques that you use.

Well, how many reservations do you think you'll get? Analyze your answers to the following questions and then make your prediction.

1. Did you attract attention and stimulate interest in your opening message through words and eye appeal (color, layout, and so on)?
2. Did you attempt to study the product and your prospective customers so that you could match your lodge facilities with their vacation needs?
3. Did you use good grammar, correct spelling, logical paragraph development, and so on, to ensure accuracy in expressing your message in your reader's language?
4. Did you talk about the lodge in an honest and believable way, and did you show *proof* of your claims?
5. Did you lead logically, using emotional appeals, to your central theme—vacationing at the Breezy Cape Lodge?
6. Did you include a specific request (preferably a positive statement or command) with a final date for registering for lodge accommodations?
7. Did you make it easy for your customers to reply to your request for early reservations?
8. Did you include a descriptive brochure illustrating the lodge facilities, and did you remember to mention it in your letter? Were the facts in the brochure and in the letter consistent?

If, in your final analysis, you can answer "yes" to the preceding questions, you will undoubtedly get more than your quota of lodge reservations!

11

Writing Problem-Solving Letters

In the American free-enterprise system, the philosophy that the customer is always right may or may not be literally true; but it should be considered true in theory. Perhaps the philosophy should be that the business worker should deal with customers in a manner that reflects that the customer is always right. Obviously, the success of a business depends upon the customer's continued satisfaction with the goods and services received.

Sooner or later, in business as well as in everyday life, somebody will err. No matter how hard we try, no matter how carefully we design, produce, inspect, and package a product, something unexpected may occur. After all, it is human to make errors. When these errors occur, as a customer you will write a claim letter asking your reader to correct his or her error; and as a business worker you will answer claims that your customers make.

Writing the Claim Letter

No matter who errs, it is always improper to write an irritable, undiplomatic letter. No one has the right to abuse another person—not even if the other person is completely in the wrong. It will never be your turn to get even. Smart business workers know that good public relations is the key to success. Millions of dollars are spent by businesses each year to relay their message to the public. It has taken several decades for good public relations to eliminate the "public be damned" image that was attributed to the industrialists of the early 1900s. It would be ridiculous to allow a hot temper to jeopardize a good public image.

When to Say "I've Got a Problem." Let's say that you ordered a blue wool blanket from a mail-order firm. The blanket has just arrived, and you discover that the company has sent you a lime-green blanket, not a blue one. Since you wish to have a blue blanket, as the color matches your room, you decide to write the mail-order firm and ask them to exchange the green blanket for a blue one.

The letter that you write to make a claim or to ask for an adjustment must possess the essential qualities of diplomacy, exactness, positiveness, and fair play. Obviously, the manner of expression should never antagonize the reader. There is no need to get angry or rude. Just as wars have never ensured peace, a loud mouth has never ensured the winning of an argument.

If you feel that you've got a problem because somebody made a mistake, it will be your responsibility to be exact and to describe the event completely by referring to the date, time, place, order number, and other pertinent information. This is no time to be vague. Also, remember that no matter how negative or unpleasant the situation is, you must withhold your emotions, placing as little emphasis as possible on the negative aspects of the situation. And you must make a reasonable claim. Lastly, in all fairness, you should give credit where credit is due! In other words, recognize the good points as well as the bad points.

Tone is important! The attitude of successful business representatives is, "If you like our service, tell others; if you don't, tell us." This reflects their desire to do right by you; when they inadvertently do something wrong, they want to be notified so they can straighten things out. As a rule, they will meet you more than halfway. They know that happy customers come back again.

Since you know and accept that they genuinely want to do what is right, you should set the mood and the tone of your letter accordingly. Therefore, if you have a routine claim message, the tone of your letter should reflect your belief that your reader wants to be told what has happened and will be eager to remedy the situation fairly.

How to Say "I've Got a Problem." In planning an adjustment request letter, you should recognize that this letter is basically a request letter. Therefore, you should apply the writing principles you learned for request letters. Make sure that you state a definite request, motivate the reader to reply to your request, and are as helpful as possible in allowing the reader to meet your request. However, you will also have to apply other principles in writing adjustment letters.

Routine claims are not serious; the reader has a clear-cut course of action to follow. For example, nobody gets too excited about exchanging a lime-green blanket for a blue one. With the more serious claim letters, there will be less chance of an automatic settlement. In such cases, you will probably have to lay the groundwork before presenting your claim. Definite appeals will have to be made, such as appeals to pride, honesty, fair play, and sometimes even fear of legal action.

A less serious appeal, naturally, is one to pride; more serious appeals would be to honesty or fair play. Of course, the most serious would be an appeal to fear of legal action, and this appeal should be a last resort. In all appeals you should remind the reader that his or her public image is at stake and that to maintain this image the reader should make a prompt adjustment.

Also, you should specifically state what adjustment you expect. Sometimes it will be to your advantage to explain when you expect such action to take place. However, act cautiously. Remember, you are to assume that you have a legitimate claim and that your reader will act promptly. This positive philosophy results in many automatic adjustments.

EXERCISE

You have been so successful in writing routine letters that you are now ready to write this unusual "I've got a problem" letter.

A little over ten months ago, your employer purchased an EXACTO desk clock and radio. After two weeks the clock stopped running every six hours or so. Since there is no local service for EXACTO timepieces in your city, you sent the clock back to EXACTO, Inc. Three months and two letters later, you got it back. But within two days, it was back to its old tricks—stopping every six hours or so. Your boss is darn angry and emphatically tells you to write a letter to EXACTO, Inc., asking them for permission to return the clock to the factory again. By the way, this time your boss wants results—not in three months but more like three days! How would you write your letter telling them about your problem? Use the following space to write your letter.

1. Did you remember to describe the situation thoroughly and to explain that you paid for a desk clock and radio more than ten months ago but still have not had the opportunity to enjoy it?
2. Did you motivate your reader by appealing to fair play?
3. Did you remember to alert your reader that EXACTO's image was at stake?
4. Did you also alert your reader to the fact that EXACTO's image could be restored by either repairing the desk clock and radio or replacing it?
5. Did you specifically inform your reader as to what action you expected?
6. Did you remember to keep your emotions intact, yet let your reader know you meant business?
7. Did your tone reflect a positive attitude by showing that you believed your reader was eager to remedy the situation and maintain your goodwill?

Answering the Claim Letter

You will also receive claim letters that you will have to answer. The requests made in claim letters will sometimes allow you to say "yes" and will at other times force you to say "no." Your job will be more difficult if you must refuse the claim or if the writer was antagonistic and belligerent. In any case, you must keep cool; you must use tact and finesse in dealing with the claim. Also, make sure that you answer promptly. Don't antagonize your reader further by delaying your answer.

When you have drafted your reply, check it carefully to make sure that your letter:

1. Possesses all the qualities of the goodwill letter.
2. Does not insinuate that the person making the claim is an agitator or a troublemaker. Avoid negative terms like "your complaint" when you could say "your letter," or like "your unfortunate experience of April 10" when you could say "the April 10 incident."
3. Gives reasonable explanations. In a letter granting the claim, include only what is absolutely necessary in the explanation; however, in a letter refusing the claim, be sure to explain before you turn down your reader's request.

The most challenging thing is to convince the customer, even if the customer is wrong, that you maintain the philosophy that the customer is always right. Your customer's rudeness does not merit your rudeness.

You should welcome this opportunity to give one of your customers personal attention.

In its own right, the adjustment letter is a goodwill letter. It may also be an opportunity to rebuild or strengthen your image. You will know what you have to say—sometimes it will be "yes" and sometimes it will be "no." It will be up to you to decide how to say it. Your goal should be *to renew a friendship.*

Answering "Yes" to the Claim Letter. The easiest type of adjustment letter you will write is the one that allows you to say "yes" to a customer's claim. However, certain precautions should be taken:

1. Don't dwell upon the problem.
2. Use inoffensive, neutral words in place of negative, offensive language.
3. Don't harangue about who is at fault. If it is you, admit it and apologize; if it isn't, just forget it. Say "yes" and end the letter.

The routine "yes" letter should include a statement that tells your reader that you are thinking alike. Remember that to the reader the most important element of the "yes" letter is the granting of the request. Thus, the "yes" letter usually will not require an explanation; granting the request will be enough to tell your reader that you are thinking alike.

In a more serious situation where the person making the claim is hostile and angry, you should attempt to smooth things out before granting the request: "Thank you for informing us that your Order 26742, dated March 15, arrived two days after your Anniversary Sale. Of course, you may return the merchandise for full credit."

Finally, you should make an attempt to regain the confidence of your customer. It is important that you sound convincing and sincere: "You will want to take advantage of the quantity discounts on White Sale items. These discounts are being offered early in July, with delivery ensured for the August white sales." Don't make impossible promises, such as "We assure you that such a thing will never happen again."

Consider the following letter:

Dear Mr. Hagerstrom:

No wonder you were confused by our billing for the expenses incurred during your July 12 Board of Directors' meeting held at our hotel. Mistakenly, we charged you for the meeting room that we said would be free.

Please deduct the $30 charge for the meeting room and send us your payment for only $142.50.

Thank you for choosing the Innwood Manor. It was a pleasure to serve you. We certainly hope that you had a successful meeting and that you will come back to the Innwood soon!

Sincerely,

This message is good because the writer admits the error and grants the customer's request for adjustment without overstressing the mistake. Notice that the writer does not promise that this will never happen again, because such a promise would be impossible to keep. The friendly closing ends the message on a positive note.

Answering "No" to the Claim Letter. There are times when it will be impossible for you to say "yes" to a claim. It may be because the article returned is a sale item, the warranty on the appliance has expired, the product has performed as well as can reasonably be expected, or someone else such as the transportation company is at fault. Sometimes it will be necessary to say "no."

This will be bad news to the reader, but you don't have to write a negative letter. Instead, use tact and other skills of effective business letter writing. It won't be necessary for you to refuse the writer outright. Imply rather than specifically state the refusal. In any case the refusal, either expressed or implied, should follow a diplomatic explanation.

Thank you for taking advantage of the Daisy Sale on January 3-9. For the protection of all our customers, swimsuits must be fitted in our store and are not exchangeable. This store policy conforms to Health Regulation Law 231.

Before discussing the "no" letter any further, let's see how you would handle the following situation.

EXERCISE

You are working for a candy manufacturing firm. One of your customers, the Parker Drugstore, ordered 150 boxes of candy in assorted sizes for the Easter season. Slow payment on the part of the Parker Drugstore forced you to write two collection letters. Finally, they sent a check for 100 boxes sold and asked if they could return the other 50 boxes for a credit of $102. Because they have given you their business for the past five years, you are not eager to lose them as a customer. But candy is a perishable item and should always be fresh and stored at room temperature. You cannot possibly do business the way they want you to. You would be encouraging customers to overorder, and you would find yourself in the position of having to accept hard, stale, dry candy. This type of service would be costly and unprofitable. Your boss has just breezed into your office and said: "That Frank Parker must be losing his mind. Why, we would have to double our prices to cover losses if we did it his way. Write to him immediately and refuse the adjustment he requests."

Write your letter in the following space—and don't forget that Frank Parker is a paying customer.

____

____

____

____

____

____

____

____

____

____

____

____

Well, how did you do? Not as easy as saying "Yes, Frank, you may return the 50 boxes of candy," was it? Evaluate your letter using the following criteria:

1. Was your overall attitude diplomatic? In other words, did you turn him down but still make him feel that you did everything possible to help him out?

2. Did you attempt to clear yourself of any blame that Mr. Parker could place on you for refusing to accept the candy?
3. Were you as positive as possible in your attempt to explain your refusal to accept the candy before actually doing so?
4. Did you imply a refusal rather than express it explicitly so as to make the refusal less painful to the customer?
5. Did you attempt to be helpful, such as by suggesting a new sales promotion idea to move the 50 boxes of candy that were not sold?
6. Did you attempt a subtle technique in your implied refusal, such as moving smoothly but rapidly to a new subject? Once again, you might have used the sales promotion idea. This technique can communicate refusal without explicitly expressing it.

Answering "Yes" and "No" to the Claim Letter. Sometimes a reply to a request letter must be a combination of saying "yes" to part of it and "no" to the other part. This letter is slightly more difficult than the letter saying "yes" and slightly less difficult than the letter saying "no." A good rule of thumb is to accent the "yes" part and play down the "no" portion of the letter.

Writing Problem-Solving Letters: A Summary

A request for an adjustment is an opportunity to get a fair settlement on a reasonable claim. A claim letter or a letter making a complaint is by its very nature unpleasant. However, the letter you write making the claim does not have to be unpleasant, especially if you do *not:*

1. Report an incident when you are highly emotional.
2. Refer to the difficulty repeatedly.
3. Use threats.
4. Give insufficient information so that the reader has difficulty interpreting the message.
5. Attempt to express "It's your fault, so what are you going to do about it?"

Of course, the letter that you write answering a claim letter must also be a pleasant communication whether you are saying "yes" or "no." The following suggestions should help you:

1. Make a decision as to what course of action you will take.
2. Write a letter that conveys this decision unambiguously.
3. Begin your letter on an agreeable note, no matter what your decision is.

4. Be kind and diplomatic, no matter how unkind or undiplomatic the writer was in making the claim.
5. Avoid an apology if there is no need for one.
6. Don't argue; it won't help.
7. Build goodwill by being as helpful as possible.

EXERCISE

As an assistant to Harry Greggus, general manager of the All-American Furniture Corporation, you are asked to reply to Mrs. Hannah York's June 12 letter.

Dear Mr. Greggus:

For more than thirty years, I have bought All-American Furniture exclusively. Until a few weeks ago, I had been very satisfied with all your products. However, the Early American rolltop desk (Model D-22) that I bought as a present for my son and daughter-in-law was damaged when it was delivered to them. The lock on the desk does not work properly—in fact, it doesn't work at all!

As a longtime customer of All-American Furniture, I expect that your company will, of course, pick up this damaged desk and replace it with a brand-new rolltop. After all, I paid more than $600 for that desk, and I certainly expect a $600 present to be in perfect condition.

Please let me know when my daughter-in-law may expect your delivery service to pick up the damaged desk and send a new one.

Sincerely,

Mr. Greggus says, "Of course, you must be sure to make every effort to keep Mrs. York as a satisfied customer and to thank her for telling us about the damaged lock. We are eager to fix the damage, but we will definitely not replace the entire desk! It's just too costly to ship two desks across the country. All we have to do is send one of our experts to her daughter-in-law's house to replace the lock with a new one. Then, the desk will be as good as new. Have the nearest authorized repair service call her no later than next week to make an appointment to fix the lock."

Write your reply to Mrs. York in the space that follows.

12

Applying for Credit

The "buy now, pay later" philosophy is in. That's why the present-day society is referred to as the "credit card crowd." Yes, the "pay-as-you-go" and "cash-and-carry" philosophies of yesterday are quite outmoded. Today, travel agencies sell vacations on credit, and cemeteries sell burial plots through a charge account system. Obviously, we have permanently moved into the credit card era.

Personal Credit

Personal credit is credit that a business or a bank grants to an individual customer, such as you. The credit card is very popular for personal or retail credit and serves as an identification at the time of purchase. The latest type of charge card is the bank credit card, such as Bank Americard and Master Charge. Merchants who honor such cards can receive an immediate payment from the bank, which acts as the clearinghouse for credit charges and collections. This type of charge card is very, very popular because it allows the small merchant the advantage of offering credit to many customers and it allows the customers with no cash to buy goods from many merchants merely on the strength of the credit card.

There are several different arrangements that can be made for personal credit. Two popular kinds of accounts are the regular charge and the revolving credit plans.

1. The regular charge account permits the customer to use an identification plate to purchase items. Usually the customer receives a statement at the end of each month, and the amount is payable on receipt of the statement. Some companies, however, use cycle billing for regular charge accounts to ensure a continuous flow of money into the firm. Billing, in other words, is done on certain days each month according to alphabetic sequence of last names. The regular charge account allows the customer the greatest credit freedom.
2. Revolving credit is the same as the regular charge account with one basic difference. The entire bill does not have to be paid upon receipt of the statement, and if it is not fully paid, a carrying charge is added to the balance. This charge may appear to be a disadvantage; however, the customer can enjoy the benefit of charging as much as he or she wishes and making only small payments.

To join the credit card crowd, the customer must make formal application. Before credit is issued, in other words, the customer usually must fill out a form. The firm granting credit will check the customer's credit rating by consulting a commercial credit book and by checking the references listed on the customer's application form.

EXERCISE

You have been purchasing many goods and services from the Dayton's catalog during the past six months and are pleased with their merchandise and service. Write to them, requesting a credit application form. Tell them you are also interested in receiving information about both their regular charge and their revolving credit plans.

Business Credit

Just as businesses extend personal credit to individuals, businesses also extend credit to other businesses. Shipping firms, manufacturers, wholesalers—all extend credit to retail businesses.

Unlike personal credit, no credit cards are used for business credit. Generally, a business writes a letter requesting that a *line of credit* be extended—that is, credit up to a specified amount. Under the terms of most credit agreements, the buyer agrees to pay the full amount of each monthly invoice within a specified time, usually thirty days. Here is a typical letter requesting credit from a wholesale drug firm:

Dear Mr. Hernandez:

In January of last year, I reopened the Wesco Drugstore on Rockaway Parkway in Westerleigh. Since then, I have been purchasing merchandise on a cash basis from several wholesale jobbers. So that I may have the opportunity to buy more economically and more conveniently, I would very much like to open an account with your firm. With your approval, I would like to establish a credit line of $1,000 with the customary terms of 2/10, n/30.

In the past ten months, the store's monthly gross income averaged $5,000. To reopen Wesco, I secured a $5,000 loan from Federal Savings and Loan on Main Street. The monthly payment on this loan is $200; the current balance is approximately $1,800. The rent for the store is $500 each month. There are no other loans or monthly obligations.

Two years ago, my husband and I purchased the one-family home at 17 Finney Road, where we now live. To buy this home, we secured a $30,000 mortgage from Westerleigh Savings and added our down payment of $15,000 to meet the purchase price. The total monthly payment for both the mortgage plus tax is $315. We have no other outstanding debts.

The following people have given me permission to use their names as references: Mr. John Aliano, Vice President, Coleman and Matzka Public Relations, Inc.; and Dr. Laura Hanks, St. Matthew's Hospital. Both are here in Westerleigh.

If you need any other information, please let me know. I look forward to establishing a mutually beneficial relationship with you.

Sincerely,

In this letter, the writer gives all the financial information that the wholesaler may need to make a decision. She asks for a specific maximum credit line of $1,000 and for standard terms—2/10, n/30—which means that (1) the buyer may deduct a 2 percent discount from the net amount if she pays within 10 days and (2) the net amount is due within 30 days.

Without these credit terms, the wholesaler would have to make the trucker responsible for collecting for each delivery to the drugstore—and there may be as many as three deliveries a week! Obviously, the wholesaler would prefer sending, and the retail drugstore would prefer paying, one monthly bill.

EXERCISE

Assume that you have been operating your own business for about six months now. You have been buying merchandise on a cash-and-carry basis from several suppliers. Now that you're settled and doing well, you'd like to establish a line of credit with one of these suppliers, Superior Products, Inc. Making up all the details, write a letter to Superior Products requesting standard credit terms. Try to make your financial statistics as realistic as possible.

Granting Credit Privileges

When a credit application or letter has been checked and approved, you will write to announce the good news. The reader will want to know immediately that credit has been granted, so why delay? Be direct and say, "Welcome—you're in!"

Your opening statement should get the relationship off to a good start by making your reader aware of being "in" as far as your family of customers is concerned. It should reflect warmth and sincerity and should welcome your new credit customer enthusiastically. Even if you have had a hard time reaching a favorable decision, you should avoid any hint of a grudging tone, stiffness, or formality.

Your letter, however, must do more than merely announce the good news. It must also build goodwill and encourage the customer to use the new credit privileges. Consider the following favorable response to a personal credit application:

Dear Miss Roth:

All of us at Wilson's are proud because you chose to become a regular charge customer of our store. We are pleased to announce that today you are listed along with almost 650,000 other charge customers and are eligible to begin charging your purchases as of tomorrow, January 10.

It is now our job to make sure that you always maintain a feeling of confidence in us. But it's my job specifically to urge everyone at Wilson's to spread out the "royal carpet" each time you come into our store.

Sincerely,

This message makes Miss Roth feel proud to be included as one of the charge customers at Wilson's. Notice also that the writer specifically states the date on which the reader can start charging her purchases.

EXERCISE

Rewrite the following "Welcome—you're in" letter granting credit privileges to a new business in your town.

Dear Ms. Jeffrey:

After checking your references, we have decided that you are a safe risk.

We certainly hope that you will accept the responsibility that goes along with getting credit—that is, making your payments within 30 days of receipt of our monthly statement. Of course, if you are a shrewd businessperson, you will take advantage of the 2 percent discount allowed on payments made within 10 days of receipt of our statements.

Since this is a special privilege given only to qualified businesses, we will expect you to adhere closely to all policies regarding your account.

Sincerely,

____

____

____

____

____

Rejecting Poor Credit Risks

Refusing credit is a more difficult situation to handle. When you say "no" to a credit applicant, you are really saying that you doubt the applicant's ability to pay his or her bills. This is a pretty serious charge. Some writers think it best to come right out and tell applicants why they are being refused credit. However, most good writers agree that the refusal should be more tactful.

In either case, the customer should be encouraged to buy on a cash basis. You can see that this will be quite a challenge for any writer whether experienced or inexperienced.

Consider the following rejection:

Dear Mr. McBride:

Unfortunately, you cannot expect to get credit at our store with your record of poor payment on other charge accounts. We have had too many unfortunate experiences with people such as you, and for this reason we have made it our company policy not to accept applications for credit from poor risks.

I'm sure you will understand why we have had to refuse your request. Thank you for applying.

Sincerely,

Obviously, this is a negative response. Even if it is honest, it isn't tactful that you state your position in such negative terms. There is no question that this customer will think twice before buying something even on a cash basis at this store after being treated so rudely.

Consider the next solution:

Dear Mr. McBride:

Thank you for applying for credit at our store. It is always a compliment to have cash customers request credit. Although we would like to grant you credit, I am afraid we cannot do so at this time.

Upon checking your references, we were told that you have unpaid balances of several months' standing at two stores. If you clear up these balances, you are eligible to make application again in six months. We will be very happy to reconsider your application at that time. Until then, we certainly hope that you will take advantage of the many sales that we will be having this summer on a cash basis.

Sincerely,

This letter is straightforward and honest, but it is also tactful and courteous. It doesn't mention anything about a lack of trust, and the last paragraph softens the refusal by suggesting an alternative.

EXERCISE

How would you answer the following letter, which was attached to Mrs. Glenda Kernan's credit application form? Your mail-order house cannot extend credit to her no matter how honest she appears to be.

I think your catalog is better than ever, and I mean it! Your bargains have saved me money, and your service has saved me time. I would like to apply for your regular charge account privileges.

Since I was graduated from college last June, I have been working as an editorial assistant for Sports magazine for $200 a week. My husband will be graduated from college next June. He already has a definite job commitment from Aldrick Imports, where he will start in September as a management trainee at a salary of $650 a month.

We pay $245.75 a month for our rent. In addition, I pay $180 a month for my student loans. My husband will start repaying his student loans next September when he starts working.

We have only one credit card, the SuperCard. Our present SuperCard balance is about $900, and our monthly payment is about $45.

We have many references as to our character. Having credit privileges at your store would certainly help us a great deal, so please consider my enclosed credit application.

Write your reply below.

Tough one to say "no" to? Sure it was. It's never easy to say "Not now—maybe later," especially when the request appears to be so honest and so necessary. You should have been very tactful when you refused this customer.

1. Did you include a statement of appreciation for the writer's request?
2. Did you honestly explain why you had to refuse the request? Did you do so before you actually refused? Sometimes this softens the actual refusal.
3. Did you make concrete, helpful suggestions as to what action she could take now?
4. Did you encourage her to continue buying on a cash basis?
5. Did you close with the hope-for-the-future attitude? Did you attempt to keep your customer's goodwill?

If you answered "yes" to the above questions, you probably lessened the blow of your refusal to this honest person's request for credit. Also, you probably retained her as a cash-paying customer—a letter-writing skill to be envied.

13

Collecting Unpaid Accounts

Whenever credit is extended to any degree, collection or pay-up letters are sure to follow. Not all promises to pay are kept. Sometimes the customer may forget to pay, may put off paying temporarily, may fail to pay because of a problem, or may just not feel like paying.

Many large companies maintain credit and collection departments to encourage customers to pay up. Obviously, profits are made through sales. Therefore, salespeople want to sign up as many customers as possible. The people who work in the credit and collection departments, however, are somewhat less enthusiastic than the salespeople about signing up customers. They move more cautiously and tend to hold out for first-rate credit customers only.

Since collection letters are usually the responsibility of credit and collection departments, you can understand why the people who must collect tend to be a little more cautious than the salespeople. The conflict between these two departments can be readily recognized. The credit and collection departments would like to have 100 percent restitution, but the sales departments frown on forceful methods of collection, because their desire is to retain the customers' business.

Collection Letter Series

It makes good sense to design collection letters with a dual purpose; namely, to collect debts and maintain goodwill—in other words, get the money and keep the customer. Even though you have the right to seek what is yours and the customer has violated the agreement, your attitude should still be that the customer is always right. You should still cater to the customer's goodwill. Therefore, you must hold anger and disgust in check. Probably the most important thing you can do in opening your letter is to encourage your reader to read it to the end.

Strictly speaking, *collection* suggests a physical act, but you will never actually *collect* money. When you plan a series of pay-up letters, your aim will be to design and organize a series of letters that will *persuade* or *sell* the reader on the idea that it will be advantageous to pay up rapidly. Avoid scolding or sermon-type discussions. They will only further antagonize or bore your reader. You should attempt to develop a program or series of letters based on the trust you had in granting the credit in the first place. Your program should attempt to persuade a delinquent customer to develop better paying habits, but at the same time it should keep the customer happy.

Persuading customers to pay up is, by its very nature, negative and reflects on personal integrity and honor. Therefore, writing collection letters will require careful planning and organization on your part.

Once the credit and collection departments recognize the delinquent accounts, they attempt to make a systematic yet flexible plan for collection. Usually the plan is to send a series of letters that get progressively more forceful. The letters are sent until payment is made. A typical letter series to persuade the customer to pay up will have four stages.

First Stage. The first stage is the notification stage. Some firms send out second and third statements, which are duplicate copies of the original. Then, if the customer does not respond, the account is declared delinquent. Once the account is considered delinquent, it is time to begin sending the collection series. A printed notice or sticker which informally requests payment may be attached to a statement, or a separate reminder may be sent. This type of reminder is usually mild and quite impersonal.

Second Stage. The second stage is a letter sent in place of the impersonal reminder. This letter is usually very mild and attempts to promote goodwill.

Third Stage. The third stage, the discussion stage, is actually the meat of the collection series. It begins when you no longer believe that the customer *will* pay. The purpose is to convince the reader that he or she *should* pay. Sometimes a series of discussion letters may be sent with each letter stressing one or more appeals designed to persuade the customer to pay up.

Fourth Stage. The fourth stage follows when the discussion stage has failed. Usually only one letter is written giving the customer a final chance to pay up before any last-resort action will be taken, such as turning the account over to a collection agency or to an attorney.

Let's look at each of the four stages in detail.

First: Notifying the Customer

Notifying your customer that his or her account is overdue is the first step in the collection series. At this stage you feel that the customer will pay; therefore, hopefully, the reminders will induce an explanation of why payment has not been made. These are always impersonal appeals; the first one may be a duplicate of the original invoice. This may be followed by a more intense effort, perhaps a statement with a rubber-stamp overdue reminder, such as:

YOUR ACCOUNT IS PAST DUE

or perhaps an invoice with an overdue-reminder sticker attached, such as:

YOUR ACCOUNT IS
__DAYS OVERDUE

Remember, these reminders are used first because you feel that the customer will pay and will do so promptly.

Second: The Pay-Up Notice or Letter

Naturally, all credit and collection departments hope that the reminders they send out will be successful, that payment will be made promptly. How easy life would be! Unfortunately, there is no question that some customers will not make restitution unless they are prodded to pay up.

Several means of communication can be used effectively. A face-to-face relationship would probably prove the most effective (if it could be arranged). Also, a telephone conversation would be more personal and effective than a letter. Both of these means would be practical only if distance were not a factor.

The letter, however, is the most common means of prodding the customer during the "customer will pay" stage. This letter is sent when impersonal reminders have failed to produce payment. The letter is mildly worded, courteous, and helpful. It may or may not be a form letter. It may be preprinted or individually typed. Because of the commonplace use of automatic typewriters and magnetic tape typewriters, the trend is toward individually typed letters rather than fill-in form letters. Examples of both follow:

Individually Typed Form Letter

Dear Dr. Svendsen:

This is to remind you that your account, No. 6742, amounting to $564.42, is now three months past due.

If you have already mailed us your check, thank you. If not, use the enclosed stamped envelope to send us your check for $564.42 today.

Sincerely,

Fill-In Form Letter

Dear ______:

This is to inform you that $_____ is now three months past due on your account, No. _____.

Please remember that your credit was granted with the understanding that payment would be made under terms of Net 30 days.

Please mail your check for $_____ in the enclosed stamped, addressed envelope today!

Sincerely,

EXERCISE

The Reynolds family of Princeton, New Jersey, engaged the Twilight Room of the Hotel Astor on January 7 for a twenty-fifth anniversary party for their parents, Mr. and Mrs. Jeremiah Reynolds. The cost of the reception, including the luncheon for 75 people, was $375. The Reynolds' oldest son, Harry, made a down payment of $100 and signed a contract to pay the balance within ten days after the reception. It is now January 18, one day past the ten-day "agree to pay" period, and you still have not received payment.

Develop a form message to remind Harry (and other customers like him) of his commitment.

____

____

____

____

Third: The "You Ought to Pay" Letter

Obviously, if you haven't heard from the customer after the reminders and the pay-up letter, you can reasonably conclude that the customer *will not* pay. It is then your responsibility to persuade the customer that he or she *ought* to pay. This stage is actually the challenge of your collection series. You must decide whether to write one "you ought to pay" letter or more than one, and you must design each for a special appeal that will induce your reader to pay up.

It will be necessary to design this letter or these letters to:

1. Arouse interest by doing something unexpected. Don't forget that the customer has received your reminders; therefore, even before opening the envelope your reader will expect an "According to our records" or "Your account is now ______ months past due." Why repeat what has already been ignored? Use a new approach. Open with a statement that will arouse interest as well as motivate a reply.
2. Motivate through carefully chosen appeals. Let such things as customer relationships, amount involved, and previous correspondence with the customer serve as your guide. Frequently used appeals are as follows:

   Fair play. Logical appeal showing how only *you* have carried out the terms of a mutual agreement.

   Ego. Emotional appeal showing that self-pride and reputation are at stake and that prompt payment can restore the reader's image.

   Sympathy. Emotional appeal telling the debtor that you need the money to keep going. This appeal is usually used when you and your debtor are good friends. It should be used with discretion, because your reader may interpret it to mean that you're in financial difficulty.

   Cooperation. Logical appeal inviting the customer to discuss the case with you. This logical appeal may be used to induce the customer to make partial payment by showing that you are open-minded and understanding and willing to cooperate.

Economy. Logical appeal showing the debtor how economy results when prompt payment is made. Prompt payment means lower operating costs, and lower operating costs mean lower customer prices.

Fear. Emotional appeal telling the debtor of drastic action that must follow—canceling credit privileges, turning the account over to a collection agency, or repossessing the goods. This appeal can be used when all others have failed.

Although the different appeals have been listed separately, you may wish to use more than one in the "customer ought to pay" letter or letters.

3. Make it clear what you expect the reader to do. If you must have full payment, make it clear. If partial payment will be acceptable, make that clear. Make sure that you restate the amount due and identify the account so the customer will have no opportunity to misinterpret what action you want him or her to take. Since the account is long past due, immediate payment is expected.
4. Help your reader to act easily. Provide physical assistance, such as a stamped, addressed envelope—anything that will serve as another reminder to pay up!

EXERCISES

1. It is now February 3, and you still have not heard from the Reynolds family. Write one "you ought to pay" letter encouraging them to clear up their unpaid account.

2. It is now March 10, and neither Harry Reynolds nor his family has made a response to any of your reminders to pay. You can reasonably conclude that they probably are not going to pay and that you are going to have to persuade them that they should pay.

   Write two letters, using a different appeal in each letter, to convince Harry that it is urgent for him to pay the balance of his account. To be effective, each letter must be personalized!

(Continued on page 130.)

Fourth: The "You Must Pay" Letter

The "you must pay" stage is the final stage in the collection series. In this stage, usually one single letter is sent to give the reader a final chance to pay before you take last-resort action, such as turning the account over to an attorney or a collection agency. Fortunately, most delinquent customers pay or make arrangements to pay before this stage is reached; occasionally, however, some "you must pay" letters have to be written.

Last-resort action for delinquent credit accounts is commonly left to a collection agency. A collection agency uses rigorous collection methods and exchanges information on delinquent customers, which could advertise customers' bad records.

You should attempt to design this final pay-up letter forcefully—with collection talk from beginning to end. Consider the following "you must pay" letter:

Dear Ms. Billings:

It's in your hands now. Yes, only you can save your credit rating and prevent legal action.

The last thing I want to do is to put your account in the hands of a collection agency. It isn't a good experience for you or for us, but I'm forced to take this action unless I receive your check for $2,438 by July 10.

Won't you help us avoid this drastic action by contacting me to discuss what you intend to do. Remember, it's in your hands now.

Sincerely,

This letter is straightforward and forceful and gives the customer one last chance to avoid the unpleasantness and expense of having her account turned over to a collection agency. This writer did not choose to review the transaction as some "you must pay" letters successfully do. Notice that the statement "It's in your hands now" sets the stage for the explanation of what such last-resort action will mean. This letter makes a final pitch for payment and sets the deadline. (The tone is as positive as it can be in such a negative situation—cool and formal, but tactful—and it should produce results.)

EXERCISE

This is it! This is the last chance for Harry Reynolds to avoid the experience of having his account put into the hands of a collection agency. Write an individualized, personal letter giving him his one last chance.

14

Preparing Employment Letters and Résumés

Since you have been promoted to a new full-time position, Mr. Turnball, your employer, has been frantically reading application letters in search of your replacement. You can't help but agree with him that the applicant whose letter and résumé appear below and on pages 133 and 139 sounds pretty good.

4217 Beachfront Road
Pasadena, CA 91103
April 29, 19—

Mr. Gerald Turnball
Assistant Sales Manager
Orange County Duplicating, Inc.
7329 Oceanview Avenue
San Francisco, CA 94132

Dear Mr. Turnball:

Will you please consider me an applicant for the part-time correspondent vacancy that you advertised in the May 10 Daily Advance.

I will be graduated from Pasadena Senior High School, Pasadena, CA 91105, on June 16, 19—, and will be ready for employment anytime after that date. While in senior high school, I maintained a perfect attendance record and a B average. During the last semester of my senior year, I was selected to be a member of the Office Education Training Program. This program utilized the latest job-training techniques, including a modern-office simulation that offered "on-the-job" experience. In this simulated office, each student rotated from one job to another, gaining experience in a variety of office roles and learning interpersonal behavior in business. In this program, I discovered my aptitude for writing, which I desire to pursue in business.

As you will notice on my enclosed résumé, I have actively participated in extracurricular activities. Probably the most challenging activity was our successful attempt to raise $2,000 to carry on our Future Business Leaders of America club activities. Club member involvement, teamwork, and responsibility have become more significant to me because of such activities.

Working as a secretary for the Vangard Insurance Company, 4500 Liberty Boulevard, Pasadena, CA 91105, my duties included typewriting, shorthand, and recordkeeping. In my job as records clerk and receptionist I learned the proper procedures for receiving and for referring callers.

Mr. Richard Loo, office manager for Vangard Insurance Company, and the others listed on my résumé have given me permission to use their names as references. You may call them or write to them for further information concerning my character and working abilities.

Will you please allow me a personal interview? If you wish, you may call me at (213) 555-2800 after 4:30 p.m.

Cordially yours,

Judith Lewis

Enclosure

How would you react to Judith's letter? Would you grant her an interview?

Judith uses one of the most effective approaches to apply for this job. She sends a résumé (a summary of her qualifications) and a letter of application. Of course, the résumé (or *data sheet,* as it is also called) and the letter are interrelated. This type of application is pleasing and inviting to read. Judith's letter is of moderate length and makes logical, psychological, and emotional appeals. Her résumé is a detailed summary of her business and educational background. The résumé is the technical rather than the personal part of the application. It is tabulated for good eye appeal.

Of all the letters that you will have to write, the letter applying for a job will be the most important to you. Your future is at stake. Success or failure here affects your future. Someday, someplace, you will want one job very badly. If the job is worth anything at all, there will be other people applying for it. You will want to put your best foot forward. You will want to look your very best. You will want to impress the reader. You will want your request to be granted.

This is the real test of your letter-writing abilities. Obviously, you will have to meet all the requirements of the particular job for which you are applying. However, just as important will be your ability to make your letter more impressive than those of the others who are applying. Someone will use your letter and résumé to judge your ability to select the facts, interpret the facts, and set your personality in writing. Your letter and résumé must sell your qualifications for the job.

Getting the Facts for Your Résumé

The first step in attempting to make a job application is to accumulate facts for your résumé. Of course, your résumé should be thorough. Don't overlook anything that is important. Keep in mind that it will be much easier for you to cut down from a large number of facts than it will be for you to add to a skimpy supply. Your résumé should include five basic categories of information:

Personal
Work experience
Education
Interests, hobbies, and achievements (or Extracurricular)
References

Take a sheet of paper or several 3 by 5 cards and list as much information as you possibly can under each of these five headings. When listing your education and work experience, use reverse chronological order; in other words, list the most recent *first.* When listing other information, place the most significant facts first. This will save you time later when you draft your résumé.

Remember that the résumé is factual and impersonal. As in the sample résumé for Judith Lewis, the writer says, "Specialized in business courses," not "*I* specialized in business courses." Incomplete sentences, then, are preferred.

Personal. List your date of birth and your physical condition (height, weight, and general health) in a form such as the following:

PERSONAL

Date of Birth: May 30, 19—
Health: Excellent Height: 5′6″ Weight: 125

NOTE: You may, if you wish, place this Personal section after your References section.

Work Experience. To have acquired work experience before being graduated from high school is impressive and is worthy of emphasis. Make a survey of your work experience. Are you presently enrolled in a cooperative part-time training program? Do you have experience as a baby-sitter or paper carrier? List each entry, beginning with your most recent position. If you have two or three to list, then omit jobs such as baby-sitter and paper carrier. Be sure to include the title of the job, the name of the employer or company, the address, and the supervisor's name and telephone number.

NOTE: If you have very little or no work experience, you may emphasize your Education and Extracurricular sections by placing both *before* your Experience section.

EXPERIENCE

Secretary, Southwest Natural Gas Company, 2142 Excelsior Boulevard, Memphis, TN 38103. September, 19—, to present. Supervisor: Mr. Roy Lind, Telephone: (901) 935-4102.
Clerk. Woolworth's, Knollwood Plaza, Chattanooga, TN 37404. June, 19—, to September, 19—. Supervisor: Mrs. Alma Ross, Telephone: (615) 938-3241.

Education. As a high school graduate, it is not necessary for you to list the elementary school or schools that you attended. If you are to be graduated in June of the year you are writing the letter, you should say "Will be graduated from Clinton High School, Clinton, Minnesota 56225, on June 4, 19—." If you have already been graduated, you can say "Was graduated from . . . ." (Do not say "Will graduate" or "Graduated from," because only an institution has the power to graduate. Say "Will *be* graduated from" or "*Was* graduated from.") You should also indicate the performance level you attained in courses that directly relate to the job. See the examples in the Education section shown below.

EDUCATION

Will be graduated from Clinton High School, Clinton, Minnesota 56225, on June 4, 19—.
Attained an A− average in business classes.
Specialized in business subjects and attained:

1. Typewriting speed of 70+ words per minute.
2. Shorthand speed of 140 words per minute.
3. Ability to operate the following business machines: Dictaphone, stencil duplicator, electric typewriter, IBM Magnetic Tape Selectric Typewriter, IBM Composer Typewriter.

Have been accepted by the College of St. Catherine, St. Paul, MN 55105.

Also, in the Education section be sure to list any special honors, awards, or achievements, such as the honor roll or the National Honor Society.

If you are listing more than one school which you have attended (not counting elementary schools), place them in reverse chronological order with the most recent school listed first.

Interests, Hobbies, and Achievements. Most employers look for well-rounded individuals, applicants who are compatible with others and who have good leadership ability. Include in your résumé any activities that will show a prospective employer that you are well rounded and that you will get along well with others.

Actually there are two types of student activities that you may list: (1) Co-curricular—those that are related directly to classroom instruction, like the vocational youth organizations (Office Education Association, Distributive Education Clubs of America, Future Business Leaders of America, Vocational Industrial Clubs of America, Future Farmers of America, and Future Homemakers of America); and (2) Extracurricular—those not directly related to classroom instruction (sports, chorus, debate, and so on). See the following example:

INTERESTS, HOBBIES, AND ACHIEVEMENTS

Vice president of the Clinton Chapter of Minnesota Office Education Association
Student secretary for Office Coordinator
Member of Donaldson's Teen Board
Junior volunteer at Fairview Hospital
Member of 19— School Yearbook staff
Hobbies of skiing and reading

References. Consider three or four references *other than relatives* who can speak well of you. Get permission from them to use their names as references *before* listing them. If the person you ask is quick to accept, you can usually assume that you've got a good reference.

Employers usually place great importance on the recommendations made by people who have seen your job performance, so if possible, be sure to list the name of someone for whom you have worked. It is also wise to list at least one member of your school staff, as employers invariably check with your school about your high school record. Include no more than one personal or character reference. When listing your references, be sure to include their complete names, describe their positions, give their business addresses, and give their telephone numbers. Make it as easy as possible for the person reading your qualifications to contact your references. Those writers who say "references provided upon request" are merely delaying their getting the job. Most employers prefer having this information on the résumé.

REFERENCES

Mrs. Edna Lansing, Engineering Manager, Eastern Construction Company, 4820 Townsend Boulevard, Johnstown, PA 15902, (612) 927-9981.

Mr. Allen Yoder, Manager, Barstow Industries, 8402 High Street, Wilkes-Barre, PA 18702, (717) 938-1170.

Once you have compiled a listing of all your qualifications and have double-checked to see that you have included all the facts and all the pertinent information, you are ready to summarize these qualifications for your résumé.

EXERCISE

Using 3 by 5 cards, list all the facts you can about yourself. As suggested previously in the chapter, use one or more cards for each of the five main headings.

Using the Facts to Write the Résumé

To be effective, the résumé must be visually attractive. It should be well organized and show an orderly presentation if it is to command the reader's attention.

Individually type each résumé on 8 1/2- by 11-inch, 20-pound, white bond paper. Never use a carbon copy! If you need more than a few copies, ask a small-job printer how much it would cost to print 50 or 100 copies.

Begin your résumé with a well-displayed heading containing your name, address, and telephone number. Then you must decide upon the overall sequence of the topics. As already stated, the order should be from the most important to the least important.

Résumé for
Judith Lewis
4217 Beachfront Road
Pasadena, California 91103
(213) 555-2800

PERSONAL

Date of Birth: August 8, 19--
Health: Excellent Height: 5'4" Weight: 115

EXPERIENCE

Secretary. Vangard Insurance Company, 4500 Liberty Boulevard, Pasadena, CA 91105. September, 19--, to present. Supervisor: Ms. Anna Robinson. Telephone: (213) 427-9530, Extension 419.
Records clerk and receptionist. Abbott, Inc., 35 Parkway Avenue, Los Angeles, CA 90032. June, 19--, to September, 19--. Supervisor: Mr. Jack Anthonie. Telephone: (213) 921-7385, Extension 42.
Kitchen aid. McCarthy's Catering, 93 West Mill Road, Pasadena, CA 91106. September, 19--, to June, 19--. Supervisor: Mr. Maurice Doher. Telephone: (213) 210-4987, Extension 2167.

EDUCATION

Will be graduated from Pasadena Senior High School, Pasadena, CA 91105, in June, 19--.
Participated in the Office Education Training Program in senior year.
Specialized in business courses and attained:

1. Typewriting speed, 60 wpm; shorthand speed, 120 wpm.
2. An understanding and operating knowledge of transcribing machines, and IBM Magnetic Tape Selectric and IBM Composer Typewriters.
3. A working knowledge of electronic calculators; ten-key adding machines; and fluid, mimeograph, and offset duplicators.
4. An understanding of human relations with co-workers and with superiors and subordinates.

Maintained a B average at Pasadena Senior High School.

EXTRACURRICULAR

Member of Pasadena Chapter of California Office Education Association (COEA).
Member of California Chapter of Future Business Leaders of America.
Chairperson of Future Business Leaders of America Fund Raising Drive to raise $2,000 for club activities.
Member of Y-Teen at Pasadena Senior High School for last two years.

REFERENCES

Mrs. Vi Gislason, Office Education Coordinator, Pasadena Senior High School, 4398 West 22 Street, Pasadena, CA 91105, (213) 431-9208.
Mr. Richard Loo, Office Manager, Vangard Insurance Company, 4500 Liberty Boulevard, Pasadena, CA 91105, (213) 427-9530.
Mrs. Martha Ellsworth, homemaker, 4120 Butterworth Heights, Pasadena, CA 91105, (213) 245-9835.
Ms. Jennifer Best, Principal, Pasadena Senior High School, 4398 West 22 Street, Pasadena, CA 91105, (213) 431-9208.

Really try to limit yourself to one page! This forces you to reevaluate your facts and delete irrelevant material. Just as lengthy letters are burdensome, so are lengthy résumés. Use a two-page résumé only if you feel you *must* to include all your qualifications.

For good eye appeal, allow ample space and use clear headings and subheadings for groups and subgroups of data. Express parallel items in a parallel manner; for example:

Member of Missouri Chapter of Distributive Education Clubs of America
Student secretary for Office Coordinator
Editor of 19— School Yearbook

You would not say in the last entry "*Was* editor of . . ." because "*Was* editor" is not parallel to "Member" and to "Student secretary." And remember to use phrases rather than sentences.

EXERCISE

Recheck your 3 by 5 cards to make sure you haven't forgotten any pertinent information. Then use these cards to draft a complete, orderly, attractive résumé. (Use the illustration on page 139 as your guide.) Check your draft for any final corrections; then type the résumé neatly on good-quality, 8½- by 11-inch paper. Limit it to one page, but make it interesting.

Using the Résumé Effectively

If your final résumé is well prepared and complete, it will serve several purposes. First, your résumé will be very helpful during an interview. Even if you have sent the interviewer your résumé, bring another copy with you to the interview. When you introduce yourself to the interviewer, you could say: "Hello, Mr. Struthers. I'm Pat Smith. I'm applying for the secretarial vacancy in the research lab. I've compiled this résumé. Maybe it can be of some help to you in our interview." And be sure to bring a copy for yourself! Second, your résumé will serve as a fact sheet that you can use to fill out the company's application form. All the dates, names, and addresses that you will need are listed in your résumé. Third, this résumé will serve as the basis for your future résumés.

Writing the Letter of Application

After you have decided on the job you would like to apply for, you should learn as much as you can about the job and the *firm*. (Can you imagine anyone applying for a job and not knowing such general facts as the location of the firm, job requirements, salary range, opportunity for advancement, and so on?) To make a preliminary investigation, call the company's personnel office (if practical in terms of distance), arrange a conversation with an employee of the firm, or read the job advertisement very carefully (some of these ads thoroughly describe the job opening). Many companies have brochures that will be helpful to you.

The more preliminary investigating you do, the more effective your letter will be and the better you will be able to sell your product—you. A blind approach to a job application can be as unsuccessful as attempting to sell a product to a public about which you know nothing. How can you write persuasively and make logical, psychological, and emotional appeals unless you know your market—the prospective employer? Your attempt to learn something about the prospective employer will show that you have initiative—a desirable characteristic for any prospective employee.

With this information and your résumé, you are ready to write a good sales letter—your letter of application. Here comes the real test of your letter-writing abilities: a descriptive, explanatory, and highly persuasive letter.

Listing the facts for your résumé forced you to accumulate much information about yourself. Getting the preliminary facts about the job and your prospective employer has provided you with information concerning the requirements of the position that you are seeking. All this vital information will help you to *match* these job requirements to the qualifications you possess.

If the letter makes such a match obvious to your reader, you will be enthusiastically considered for an interview. After all, you are in demand. The employer needs you if you can do the job. Your résumé can serve as the job-qualification fact sheet; however, it should be your *letter* that will sell your prospective employer on the fact that you have the qualifications necessary to fill the job. The match must be made obvious; it cannot be left to chance. Your letter must tell exactly how your qualifications actually meet the job requirements.

You must sell your reader on your product—you. In the letter of application, match your qualifications to the employer's needs. With this approach, you are bound to land the job!

The Format of the Letter. Will you succeed in convincing your prospective employer that you are the best person for the job? To be sure you do succeed, follow these suggestions in writing your letter:

1. Attract favorable attention by:

   a. Taking pains with the physical appearance and arrangement of the letter (stationery, typing, paragraphing, grammar, punctuation, spelling, and so on).
   b. Explaining how you learned of the vacancy, if possible.
   c. Indicating the exact purpose of the letter.

   Mrs. Janice Sullivan, my office coordinator, has informed me of a secretarial vacancy in your firm. Will you please consider me an enthusiastic applicant?

2. Create desire or interest by:

   a. Stating and then analyzing the major requirements of the position you have in mind.
   b. Showing conclusively that your education, training, and experience specifically meet these requirements. Remember that your résumé is attached to the letter and should be referred to throughout the letter. It isn't necessary, however, for you to repeat in your letter all the facts that are on your résumé. Consistently *lead* the reader into the résumé for actual facts.

   As you will see on my enclosed résumé, since last year I have been working part-time as a clerk-typist for DataTronics, Inc.

3. Convince the employer that you are the person for the job by:

   a. Supplementing the statement already made with a presentation of those personal qualifications or characteristics that seem most desirable.

   During my senior year, I was elected vice president of the Miami Chapter of the Future Business Leaders of America. By working to gain the support and team effort of my peers, I have become conscious of the importance of good human relations. This awareness should make me a more qualified and perceptive secretary.

   b. Showing genuine interest in the business, together with an expression of confidence in your ability to adapt your particular training to meet the employer's requirements.

c. Suggesting, if it seems appropriate, your ultimate career goal, as well as your immediate objective.
d. Reassuring the employer that you don't want just work, but rather the chance to tackle a given problem and solve it.

4. Stimulate action by:

a. Offering references that will vouch for your experience, education, and character.
b. Requesting an interview.
c. Supplying the employer with the information necessary to arrange the interview.

To arrange an interview at your convenience, please call me at DataTronics from 3 p.m. to 6 p.m. any day from Monday through Friday.

The Beginning of the Letter. The first paragraph of the letter of application should immediately arouse the reader's attention. If the letter fails here, it usually fails in its ultimate purpose—to get you an interview. Most employers judge the ability of an applicant by the degree of excellence of this letter.

Your first paragraph should suggest your individuality. Avoid trite, hackneyed beginnings, and do not be too radical, eccentric, or artificial. The beginning should reveal the purpose of your letter and indicate how you learned about the position. Do not be vague. Do not leave it to the reader to guess the purpose of your letter.

EXERCISE

Write the first paragraph of a letter of application for each of the following situations. In each case, fill in the specific details required.

1. Assume that a friend—not known to the reader—told you about a job opening in a company for which you would like to work.

___

___

___

(Continued on page 144.)

2. Assume that a friend of yours—an expert who is well known in your field and is highly respected by the reader—told you about the job.

The Middle of the Letter. In the middle section of your letter, develop the relation of your education and experience (if you have any) to the requirements of the position. To stress your best selling points, place them in the most prominent position.

In the middle section, be sure to include:

1. A presentation of the particular requirements of the position.
2. A detailed account of your education and your practical work experience.
3. A convincing statement *matching* your particular qualifications to the specific requirements of the position. (This is the *match* we discussed, and it is probably the most important part of your letter. It shows why you have an interest in the position.)

Your letter must reveal your ambition, your determination, and your abilities. Your positive traits and skills are what the employer is looking for. If your interests and hobbies describe you better than anything else, then use them to describe yourself. But do not make the body of the letter too long or involved. Each paragraph should emphasize a particular selling point. Sentences should be clear and to the point. Avoid all irrelevant material.

The End of the Letter. The end or conclusion of your letter of application has a twofold purpose—to request an interview and to make it easy for the reader to grant that interview. Leave no doubt in the reader's mind of your desire for an interview. State definitely and completely how and when you may be reached. Give as much attention to the individuality and the force of your ending as you do to the beginning of your letter.

EXERCISE

From the want ads in your local newspaper, choose a job for which you would like to apply and for which you are qualified. If you prefer, you may choose as your potential job an opening described to you by a friend. In either case, get as many facts as possible about the potential job and the employer. Then, using the résumé you prepared, write a persuasive letter of application.

Type your letter of application on plain bond paper, 8½ by 11 inches. Do not use printed letterhead for letters of application.

Writing a Follow-Up Letter

After an interview, some applicants write a letter to thank the interviewer. People who conduct interviews admit frankly that they are impressed when they receive such letters and that they don't receive enough of them. Obviously, you probably won't be considered for the job just because you wrote it, but your follow-up letter could have some bearing in a very close contest between you and another applicant.

This letter must be prompt and sincere. It should be written on the same day as the interview or no later than the day following the interview. It should reach the reader before he or she has made a decision.

Here is an example of a follow-up letter:

> **Thank you for allowing me to talk to you in person about my qualifications for the secretarial position in your Research Department.**
>
> **Also, I certainly appreciated meeting your president, Mrs. Davidson. It is understandable why your firm has enjoyed such success.**
>
> **This experience made me even more eager to be in your employment and to learn of your decision.**

This letter is not gushy. Appropriately, it shows appreciation for having been granted an interview (not for the time spent in the interview) and for having been introduced to the president.

EXERCISE

Yesterday you had an interview with Mrs. Agatha Cushing, personnel manager for Cardinal Industries. She told you that although no jobs were now available, she would be glad to have you call again in two or three months. As you left her office, Mrs. Cushing gave you a booklet describing the company and its products. Write a letter thanking her for the interview in a way that will make her think favorably of you and will remind her of you when a person with your qualifications is needed. Such letters are interpreted as evidence of good manners.

Writing a Letter of Resignation Another employment letter that you may have to write is a resignation letter. As a business worker you must give your employer formal notice that you plan to leave the company, and you should give this notice at least two weeks before you will leave. Look at the illustration below.

Dear Mr. Brooks:

Please accept my resignation as executive secretary for the Research Department effective June 10, 19—.

Since I plan to move to Denver, Colorado, on July 1, I will need a few weeks to get things ready and packed. If you wish, I will be happy to train my replacement.

Thank you for the opportunity to work with your Research Department. This job allowed me to expand my experience and thus become a more perceptive secretary. My replacement has much to look forward to!

Respectfully yours,

This letter of resignation:

1. Is brief and to the point.
2. States the specific date of termination.
3. States the reasons for terminating employment. (You should use tact in stating reasons. For instance, you should not say, "I am taking a position with the Spoon River Company because it pays more money." "Personal advancement" is one acceptable reason that is noncommittal.)
4. Mentions that working with the company has been enjoyable.
5. Uses an appropriate complimentary close, "Respectfully yours."

15 Preparing Reports

In the modern business world, report writing plays a vital role. Business report writing is similar to business letter writing. Both must be fitted to your reader's needs. Both must be accurate and easy to read. Most reports are prepared in answer to specific requests for information. Visualize the report as an effort to size up a specific situation and to deliver information to someone who is in need of it (this includes your superiors, co-workers, and perhaps those working for you). Reports can be oral or written, formal or informal. Our main interest here is the written report—especially the informal written report, because it is so commonly used in business today.

As an office worker, you will be faced with the task of preparing periodic reports or progress reports. You will be writing either information reports, which merely present facts, or the more sophisticated analytical reports. In an analytical report, you will be required to interpret the facts for the reader and in some instances to suggest one or more remedies to a problem.

First of all, you must define your problem and state it in the title of your report. Second, you should gather the facts that will be needed to reach a solution. This could mean examining sales statistics, comparing estimates, preparing schedules, and so on. Next, you should analyze the data collected. Obviously, such things as sorting, coding or classifying, computing, and tabulating are commonly required in this step. Finally, on the basis of careful evaluation, you should select the method in which you will present your information. All these steps must be taken before you are ready to draft your report.

Writing Informal Reports

Most of the reports that you will write will simply provide factual information about a subject. These informal reports are most common when research is light and where content is brief. The two formats for informal reports are the *memorandum* (used for communications within the company) and the *letter* (used for communications to other companies). A sample memorandum report appears on page 151. The letter report contains all the elements of a regular business letter—heading, inside address, salutation, body, closing, and signature.

When you prepare an informal report, using either the memorandum or the letter format, you may wish to make a continuous flow of the content of the text; or if it is too lengthy or cumbersome, you may wish to attach separate sheets to the report in the form of enclosures. This will depend on the length and the nature of your information. You will also have to choose either a personal tone (*I*, *you*) or an impersonal tone (*the writer* and *the reader* instead of *I* and *you*), depending on your reader. The personal tone is usually preferred.

Whether your report is a letter or a memorandum, you will have to decide how you are going to present your information. You may wish to present your data in alphabetical order, order of importance, chronological order—whichever serves your purpose best.

1. **Alphabetical order.** If you were asked, for example, to prepare an up-to-date list of the service centers that your company operates throughout the country, you might arrange your information as follows:

Abilene, Texas 79603
    Abilene Appliance Center, 112 Main Street
Albany, New York 12210
    Capitol Service, 8 Utica Avenue
Albuquerque, New Mexico 87111
    Southwest Appliance Service, 1162 Sunset Highway

Baltimore, Maryland 21215
Authorized Service Center, 432 Route 79
Better Service Center, 80 Avenue T
Canton, Ohio 44702
Professional Appliance Services, 57 Lowell Boulevard

2. **Order of importance.** If, for example, you were asked to compare the sales of various products for one full year, you might arrange your data according to their importance—that is, according to their dollar sales:

Product	Unit Sales	Dollar Sales
UltraJoy Liquid Cleaner (quart), $1.98	96,241	$190,557
Brite Shine Polish, $1.69	82,431	138,308
UltraJoy Liquid Cleaner (gallon), $4.98	26,642	132,677
Silver-Glo Spray, $2.29	51,439	117,795

3. **Chronological order.** Say, for example, that your company advertises in several monthly magazines. The advertising manager wants to know exactly how many of the coupon order forms that accompany these ads have been received for each magazine ad since the beginning of this year. You decide to present the information in chronological order:

Month	Fun Magazine	RSVP Magazine	Realities Magazine	Monthly Total
January	65	78	94	237
February	56	83	106	245
March	89	57	86	232
April	98	87	94	279
TOTAL	308	305	380	993

Notice the following example of a routine information report. This particular report lists the information in chronological order.

TO: Daniel Evans **FROM:** Pat Kramer

SUBJECT: Estimated Sales Compared With Actual Sales for <u>The Art of Writing Effective Letters, Second Edition</u> **DATE:** June 12, 19—

In answer to your June 9 request, I have compared the estimated sales figures with the actual sales figures for <u>The Art of Writing Effective Letters</u>, by Stein and Robinson, since its publication.

Sales	19—	19—	19—	19—	TOTAL
Number of copies					
Estimated	10,000	11,000	10,500	10,000	41,500
Actual	7,800	14,000	13,800	15,000	50,600
Dollar revenue					
Estimated	$60,000	$66,000	$63,000	$60,000	$249,000
Actual	$46,800	$84,000	$82,800	$90,000	$303,600

Although actual sales fell below estimated sales for the first year, actual sales were greater than estimated sales for each succeeding year. Thus the total actual sales to date exceeds estimated sales by 9,100 copies, or $54,600.

Please let me know if you would like to see a complete profit study for this edition or a comparison of sales with the previous edition.

This is an effective informal report because:

1. The subject is clearly stated in the first paragraph.
2. It gives the reader the information requested. It contains no irrelevant information and offers to provide more information if the reader wishes it.
3. It presents the information in an easy-to-understand manner. The tabular display makes it easy for the reader to compare estimated sales with actual sales for each year. Presenting the information in sentence form would have made it more difficult to compare these figures.
4. The use of the pronouns *I*, *you*, and *me* gives it a direct but personal flavor.

EXERCISE

Your employer, Miss Libby Frank (whom you call by her first name), asks you to prepare a report of the employment anniversary dates of those employees of the Accounting Department whose employment anniversaries fall during the second half of the year. To get this information you search the personnel files and secure the following information:

Roosevelt Brown, a payroll clerk, was hired 4 years ago on August 23; Janis Johnson, a billing clerk, has been with the company for 18 years and was hired on November 19; Myron Shapiro, an accounts receivable clerk, started with the company 7 years ago on October 6; Lawrence Laguri, an accounts payable clerk, will celebrate his 10th anniversary with the company on December 29.

On a separate sheet of paper, write an informal memorandum report to Miss Frank, presenting this information in a clear, easy-to-understand manner. Be sure to include the headings *To*, *From*, *Subject*, and *Date*, as in the memorandum on page 151.

Writing Formal Reports

You will, on occasion, be asked to present a formal report. The informal report is, as you have seen, a simple, straightforward, easy-to-write, personal piece of correspondence. The formal report, on the other hand, is a complicated, lengthy, time-consuming, and impersonal analysis of a problem. Unlike the informal report, the formal report is not a routine piece of correspondence. The formal report is usually written in the third person. A letter or memo of transmittal accompanies the report; it varies in length and actually says, "Here is the report you asked me to prepare."

Because of the complexity and the length of this report, it is generally divided into the following parts.

Title Page. This is the first page of the formal report and usually includes four things: the title, the name of the person receiving the report, the author, and the date the report is submitted. Of course, all these things should be arranged attractively. Never type a page number on a title page. The title is usually centered in capital letters and should be as concise as possible. If more than one line is required for the title, the lines should be arranged in an inverted pyramid style, such as:

A COMPARATIVE ANALYSIS OF THE DUTIES
OF THE CLERK AND THE SECRETARY

Preface. The preface is an introductory discussion. In it, the author may give background material, reasons for undertaking the project, the method of conducting research, and so on. A roman numeral is used to number the preface page.

Table of Contents. This is a list of what will follow in the text of the report. The contents includes the titles of the sections of the report and of the major headings within each section. Each section and heading title is typed on a separate line. As in the table of contents of a printed book, a corresponding page number is typed next to each line to show where that section begins. A roman numeral is also used on each page of the table of contents.

List of Illustrations. The list of illustrations helps the reader locate visual and graphic aids by listing the page numbers on which they appear. Again, a roman numeral is used to number this page.

Synopsis. The synopsis is a summary of the text. Its length may vary, but it should include a statement of the problem, your findings, and your conclusions or recommendations. The purpose of placing the summary before the actual text is to rapidly relay the message of the report to your reader. This section, too, is paginated in roman numerals.

Body or Text. This is the main section of the formal report. Here the subject is explained and analyzed. An introduction, including a statement of the purpose of the report and perhaps the methods used in gathering facts, opens the body of the report. This is followed by a discussion, an analysis, and a presentation of the facts. A conclusion or summary ends this part of the report.

Beginning with the body or text, arabic numbers will be used throughout the rest of the report. Since the rules of typing reports state that no number is typed on the first page, start with arabic numeral *2* on the second page of the report.

Appendix. This supplementary section contains graphic aids that would be too cumbersome if inserted in the body of the report. However, reference to them should be made in the report. Material that is less than one-half of a page should be included in the text rather than in the appendix. The reader should not be asked to flip to the appendix for constant reference.

Bibliography. The bibliography is a list of the books and periodicals used as sources of information in writing the report. For each entry, include the author's name, the title of the article, the name of the book or periodical, the volume and issue number, the name of the publisher, the place of publication, and the date of publication. This listing should be in alphabetical order by authors' surnames.

Index. The index, the final supplementary section, is an alphabetical listing of the significant names, topics, and subtopics contained in the report, together with a notation of the pages on which each appears throughout the report.

For a guide to typing your report, see *Reference Manual for Stenographers and Typists, Fourth Edition*, by Ruth E. Gavin and William A. Sabin, McGraw-Hill, New York, 1970.

Reference Section

Always make sure that your written messages meet the standards of modern business correspondence. Whenever you are uncertain whether your punctuation, number, abbreviation, or capitalization style is correct, find the right answer in an authoritative source. The short time that it will take you to do so will be well worth the effort!

This Reference Section includes a summary of the most commonly used principles of punctuation, number, abbreviation, and capitalization styles for business writing. Read this section to become acquainted with these principles, and refer to it whenever you must. For a complete manual on grammar, usage, and style, see *Reference Manual for Stenographers and Typists, Fourth Edition,* by Ruth E. Gavin and William A. Sabin.* The material in this Reference Section has been condensed from that book.

At the end of the Reference Section (pages 169 and 170) are illustrated a few samples of the business-letter styles most commonly used in modern offices: the full-blocked, blocked, semiblocked, and simplified letter styles. Use these samples to guide you in preparing your business letters.

PUNCTUATION

The Period

1. Use a period to mark the end of a sentence that makes a statement or expresses a command.

We are eager to hear your report. (Statement.)

Be sure to return the contract promptly. (Command.)

2. Use a period to mark the end of an indirect question.

The main question is whether the job will be completed on schedule.

Who the new director will be has not yet been announced.

The Question Mark

1. Use a question mark at the end of a direct question.

Where are the records for Frasier, Inc.?

Why not make an appointment today?

2. Use a question mark at the end of a sentence that is phrased like a statement but spoken with the rising intonation of a question.

They still doubt our figures?

This total is correct?

3. A series of brief questions at the end of a sentence may be separated by commas or (for emphasis) by question marks. Do not capitalize the individual questions.

Can you estimate the cost of the roofing, the tile work, and the painting?

OR: **Can you estimate the cost of the roofing? the tile work? the painting?**

The Exclamation Point

1. Use an exclamation point at the end of a sentence (or an expression that stands for a sentence) to indicate enthusiasm, surprise, incredulity, urgency, or strong feeling.

Yes! Dresses, jackets, and coats are selling at 50 percent off!

*Ruth E. Gavin and William A. Sabin, *Reference Manual for Stenographers and Typists*, 4th ed., Gregg Division, McGraw-Hill Book Company, New York, 1970.

2. A single word may be followed by an exclamation point to express intense feeling. The sentence that follows it is punctuated as usual.

Wait! We can't sign this agreement.

3. When such words are repeated for emphasis, an exclamation point follows each repetition.

Hush! Hush! Don't let this secret out.

The Comma

The comma has two primary functions: it *separates* elements within a sentence to clarify their relationship to one another, and it *sets off* parenthetical elements that interrupt the flow of thought. It takes only a single comma to "separate," but it typically requires two commas to "set off."

1. *In Compound Sentences.* When a compound sentence consists of two independent clauses joined by *and*, *but*, *or,* or *nor*, a "separating" comma should precede the conjunction.

We talked for twenty minutes, *and* then we showed our slides.

The material in this coat is not the right color, *nor* is it the quality ordered.

2. If the two clauses of a compound sentence are short, the comma may be omitted before the conjunction.

Their prices are low and they offer good service.

Please sign these forms and return them by tomorrow.

3. *In Complex Sentences.* A complex sentence contains one independent clause and one or more dependent clauses. *After*, *although*, *as*, *because*, *before*, *if*, *since*, *unless*, *when*, and *while* are among the words most frequently used to introduce dependent clauses.

4. When a dependent clause *precedes* a main clause, separate the two clauses with a comma.

***Before you decide,* please read this.**

5. When a dependent clause *follows* the main clause or *falls within* the main clause, commas are used or omitted depending on whether the dependent clause is essential (restrictive) or nonessential (nonrestrictive).

a. An *essential* clause is necessary to the meaning of the sentence. Because it *cannot be omitted*, it should not be set off by commas.

This schedule is for everyone *who works in the plant*. (Tells which persons.)

Ben said *that the total was incorrect*. (Tells what was said.)

b. A *nonessential* clause provides additional descriptive or explanatory detail. Because it *can be omitted* without changing the meaning of the sentence, it should be set off by commas.

We stopped off in Denver to see our partner, *who is an eminent author*. (Simply adds information about the partner.)

c. A dependent clause occurring within a sentence must always be set off by commas when it interrupts the flow of the sentence.

We can schedule the meeting for tomorrow or, *if you prefer*, for Friday.

6. *With Participial, Infinitive, and Prepositional Phrases*. Use a comma after an *introductory participial phrase*.

***Speaking in a loud voice*, Mrs. Earnest called the meeting to order.**

7. Use a comma after an *introductory infinitive phrase* unless the phrase is the subject of the sentence. (Infinitive phrases are introduced by the word *to*.)

***To obtain the best results from the camera*, read all the directions.**

8. Use a comma after an *introductory prepositional phrase* unless the phrase is short and no misunderstanding is likely to result from the omission of the comma.

> ***In response to the many requests of our customers,* we are opening a suburban branch. (Comma required after a long phrase.)**

9. *With Introductory, Parenthetical, or Transitional Expressions.* Use commas to set off parenthetical elements—that is, words, phrases, or clauses that are not necessary to the completeness of the structure or the meaning of the sentence. Such expressions either provide a transition from one thought to the next or reflect the writer's attitude toward the meaning of the sentence.

> ***After all,* we have revised these estimates twice.**
>
> **It is clear, *however,* that we must increase our weekly quota.**

10. *In a Series.* When the last member of a series of three or more items is preceded by *and*, *or*, or *nor*, place a comma before the conjunction as well as between the other items.

> **Study the rules for the use of the comma, the semicolon, *and* the colon.**

11. *With Adjectives.* When two or more consecutive adjectives modify the same noun, separate the adjectives by commas.

> **The agency described her as a *quiet, efficient* worker. (A worker who is quiet and efficient.)**

12. *With Identifying, Appositive, or Explanatory Expressions.* Words, phrases, and clauses that identify or explain other terms should be set off by commas.

> **Pat Clark, *our supervisor,* is retiring on Monday, June 30.**

13. *With Interruptions of Thought and Afterthoughts.* Use commas to set off words, phrases, or clauses that interrupt the flow of a sentence or that are loosely added at the end as an afterthought.

> **She has approved, *so I was told,* the site for our convention.**

14. *To Indicate Omitted Words.* Use a comma to indicate the omission of a word or words that are clearly understood from the context. (The omitted words are usually verbs.)

> **Sandra Lopes manages our California office; Sal Margot, our Florida office.**

15. *In Direct Address.* Names and titles used in direct address must be set off by commas.

> **All of us wish you success, *Mrs. Oakley,* in your new position.**

16. *In Dates.* Use two commas to set off the year when it follows the month and day or the month alone.

> **We introduced this new product to potential investors on January 2, 1976, as we were scheduled to.**

17. *With States and Countries.* Use two commas to set off the name of a state, a country, a county, etc., that directly follows a city name.

> **You can fly from Miami, *Florida,* to Bogotá, *Colombia,* in under four hours.**

18. *With* Jr., Sr., *Etc.* Use commas to set off designations following a person's name, such as *Jr., Sr., Esq.,* and abbreviations signifying academic degrees or religious orders.

> **Mr. L. B. Kelly, *Jr.*, sailed for Europe today. (A growing trend in business correspondence is to omit the commas with *Jr.* and *Sr.*)**
>
> **We were represented in court by Marion Stevens, *Esq.*, of New York.**

19. *With* Inc. *and* Ltd. Insert a comma before *Inc.* and *Ltd.* in company names unless you know that the official name of the company is written without a comma. Within a sentence, a comma must follow the abbreviation if a comma also precedes it.

Scarpa Shoes, Ltd. BUT: **Time Inc.**

20. *In Figures.* When numbers run to four or more figures, use commas to separate thousands, hundreds of thousands, millions, etc.

$2,375.88 **147,300**

21. Do not use commas in year numbers, page numbers, house or room numbers, telephone numbers, serial numbers (for example, invoice, style, model, or lot numbers), and decimals.

1973 **8760 Sunset Drive** **846-0462**

The Semicolon

1. When a coordinating conjunction (*and, but, or,* or *nor*) is omitted between two independent clauses, use a semicolon—not a comma—to separate the clauses.

The sales estimate was low; the manufacturing estimate was high.

a. Use a semicolon to achieve a stronger break between clauses than a comma provides.

All of us are convinced that we will complete the project well before the end of next year; but no one is willing to guarantee that the final cost will be within the budget.

b. Use a semicolon when one or both clauses contain internal commas and a misreading might occur if a comma were also used to separate the clauses.

We sent you an order for bond letterheads, onionskin paper, carbons, and envelopes; and shipping tags, cardboard cartons, stapler wire, and binding tape were sent to us instead.

2. When independent clauses are linked by transitional expressions, use a semicolon between the clauses. (If the second clause is long or requires special emphasis, treat it as a separate sentence.)

The suggestion was accepted; *moreover,* it was accepted without any debate.

3. In general, when two independent clauses are linked by a transitional expression such as *for example* (abbreviated *e.g.*), *namely,* or *that is* (abbreviated *i.e.*), use a semicolon before the expression and a comma afterward.

He is highly qualified for the job; *for example,* he has had ten years' experience in the field.

4. Use a semicolon to separate items in a series if any of the items already contains commas.

The members of the panel were Elaine Osgood, executive vice president; Donald Berkowitz, marketing director; Cynthia Lindstrom, advertising manager; and Paul Hingle, sales promotion manager.

5. Use semicolons to separate a series of parallel subordinate clauses if they are long or contain internal commas. (However, a simple series of dependent clauses requires only commas, just like any other kind of series.)

She suggested that we should review the existing specifications, costs, and sales estimates for the project; that we should analyze Bartlett's alternative figures; and that we should prepare a detailed comparison of the two proposals.

The Colon

1. Use a colon between two independent clauses when the second clause explains or illustrates the first clause and there is no coordinating conjunction or transitional expression linking the two clauses.

The position you have described sounds very attractive: the salary is good and the opportunities for advancement seem excellent.

2. Place a colon before such expressions as *for example, namely,* and *that is* when they introduce words, phrases, or a series of clauses anticipated earlier in the sentence.

The secretary of the committee has three important duties: *namely,* to attend all meetings, to write the minutes, and to send out notices.

3. When hours and minutes are expressed in figures, separate the figures by a colon, as in the expression *8:25*.

4. A colon is used to represent the word *to* in proportions, as in the ratio *2:1*. (No space precedes or follows this colon.)

5. In business letters, use a colon after the salutation. In social letters, use a comma.

The Dash

1. Use the dash to set off a parenthetical element that requires special emphasis.

We must make sure that our agents—as well as the transportation companies and the public—are notified of this trend.

2. Use a dash to show an abrupt break in thought or to set off an afterthought.

Here's gourmet food in a jiffy—economical too!

3. Use dashes to set off single words that require special emphasis.

Money—that is all he thinks about.

4. Use dashes to set off and emphasize words that repeat or restate a previous thought.

Right now—at this very moment—our showrooms are crammed with bargains.

5. Use a dash before such words as *these, they,* and *all* when these words stand as subjects summarizing a preceding list of details.

Economical, efficient, and durable—these are the qualities of the Eager lawn mower.

Parentheses

1. Use parentheses to enclose explanatory material that is independent of the main thought of the sentence.

We are disappointed at the very small number of orders (five) we received today.

2. Use parentheses to set off references and directions.

Since our expenses to date have been unusually heavy (see the financial report attached), we must curtail our spending for the rest of the year.

3. Dates that accompany a person's name or an event are enclosed in parentheses.

Susan B. Anthony (1820-1906) was the subject of the film.

4. Use parentheses to enclose numbers or letters that accompany enumerated items within a sentence.

We need the following information to complete our order: (1) the list price of this product, (2) the minimum quantity that must be ordered, and (3) the credit terms available.

Quotation Marks

1. Use quotation marks to enclose a *direct quotation,* that is, the exact words of a speaker or a writer.

"Please revise the last paragraph in that letter," said Mr. Levi.

2. When only a word or phrase is quoted from another source, place quotation marks around only the words *taken from the original source.*

Miss Como said she would decide when she had "all the facts." (Miss Como's exact words were, "I will decide when I have all the facts.")

3. Words used humorously or ironically are enclosed in quotation marks.

It's "genuine" all right—a genuine imitation!

4. Slang or poor grammar that is purposely used is enclosed in quotation marks.

Whatever the secret may be, Jeff "ain't sayin'."

5. Words and phrases introduced by such expressions as *so-called, marked, signed,* and *entitled* are enclosed in quotation marks.

The carton was marked "Fragile."

6. Use quotation marks around titles that represent only *part* of a complete published work—for example, chapters, lessons, topics, sections, parts, tables, and charts within a book; articles and feature columns in newspapers and magazines; and essays, short poems, lectures, and sermons.

When you read Chapter 5, "Effective Business Letters," give special attention to the section headed "Qualities of Effective Letters."

7. Use quotation marks around the titles of *complete but unpublished* works, such as manuscripts, dissertations, and reports.

Please order a copy of Homelka's study, "Criteria for Evaluating Personnel."

8. Use quotation marks around titles of songs and other short musical compositions, titles of paintings and pieces of sculpture, and titles of television and radio series and programs.

Everyone sang "Happy Birthday" to him.

9. A quotation within another quotation is enclosed in single quotation marks.

"Once again, this style is 'in' in the fashion world."

10. *Periods* and *commas* always go *inside* the closing quotation mark.

Ms. Belov said, "Please pay for this out of petty cash."

The Underscore

1. A word referred to as a word is usually underscored (or italicized in print), but it may be enclosed in quotation marks instead. A word referred to as a word is often introduced by the expression *the term* or *the word.*

The words <u>stationary</u> and <u>stationery</u> have quite different meanings. (ALSO: The words "stationary" and "stationery" have quite different meanings.)

2. In a formal definition the word to be defined is usually underscored and the definition is usually quoted.

The term <u>psychosomatic</u> has an interesting derivation: the prefix <u>psycho</u> means "of the mind"; the root word <u>soma</u> refers to the body.

3. Underscore foreign expressions that are not considered part of the English language. (Use quotation marks to set off the translations.)

A <u>faux pas</u> literally means a "false step."

4. Underscore titles of *complete* works, such as books, pamphlets, long poems, magazines, and newspapers. Also underscore titles of movies, plays, musicals, operas, and long musical compositions.

Please order a copy of <u>Human Relations and Motivation</u> for our library.

The Apostrophe

1. The apostrophe is used to form the possessive of nouns and certain pronouns.

employee's record **one's choice**

2. The apostrophe is used to indicate the omission of a letter in a contraction.

doesn't **we're**

3. The apostrophe may be used to form the plural of letters, figures, symbols, etc., if the plural might otherwise be confused. If no confusion will result, the apostrophe is unnecessary.

PTAs **1900s** BUT: **dotting the i's**

4. The apostrophe is used to indicate the omission of the first part of a date.

class of '77

CAPITALIZATION

1. Capitalize the first word of (**a**) every sentence, (**b**) an expression used as a sentence, (**c**) a quoted sentence, and (**d**) an independent question within a sentence.

Up-to-date statistics will be available tomorrow.

So much for that. **Really?** **No!**

Their representative said, "Our estimates will be submitted on Monday."

The question is, Will this policy improve employee morale?

2. Capitalize the first word of each item displayed in a list or an outline and the first word of each line in a poem. (Always follow the style of the poem itself, however.)

3. Capitalize every proper noun, that is, the official name of a particular person, place, or thing. Also capitalize adjectives derived from proper nouns.

George (n.), Georgian (adj.)

South America (n.), South American (adj.)

4. Capitalize imaginative names and nicknames of particular persons, places, or things.

the First Lady **the Windy City**

5. Capitalize a common noun when it is an actual part of a proper name. However, do not capitalize the common-noun element when it is used in place of the full name.

Professor Burke BUT: **the professor**
the Chase Corporation **the corporation**

6. Capitalize all official titles of honor and respect when they *precede* personal names.

Professor Ella McCann **Dr. Morgan**

Mayor Pat Loo **Ambassador Franklin**

7. In general, do not capitalize titles of honor and respect when they *follow* a personal name or are used *in place of* a personal name.

Dr. Arthur Orwell, *president* of Cromwell University, will speak tonight at eight. The *president's* topic is . . . .

8. Capitalize words such as *mother, father, aunt, uncle,* etc., when they stand alone or are followed by a personal name.

I called *Mother* and *Dad* last night.

9. Capitalize the names of companies, associations, societies, independent committees and boards, schools, political parties, conventions, fraternities, clubs, and religious bodies. (Follow the style used by the organization in its letterhead or other written communication.)

the Anderson Hardware Company
the Young Women's Christian Association

10. Common organizational terms such as *advertising department, manufacturing division, finance committee,* and *board of directors* are ordinarily capitalized when they are the actual names of units within the writer's own organization. These terms are not capitalized when they refer to some other organization, unless the writer has reason to give these terms special importance or distinction.

The *Board of Directors* will meet on Thursday at 2:30. (From a company memorandum.)

BUT: **Edward Perez has been elected to the *board of directors* of the Kensington Corporation. (From a news release.)**

11. Capitalize *the* preceding the name of an organization only when it is part of the legal name of the organization.

The Investment Company of America

12. Capitalize the names of countries and international organizations as well as national, state, county, and city bodies and their subdivisions.

the Republic of Panama
the Ohio Legislature

13. Capitalize short forms of names of national and international bodies and their major divisions.

the House (referring to the House of Representatives)

14. Capitalize *federal* only when it is part of the official name of a federal agency, a federal act, or some other proper noun.

the *Federal* Reserve Board

BUT: **. . . subject to federal, state, and local laws.**

15. Capitalize the names of places, such as streets, buildings, parks, monuments, rivers, oceans, and mountains. Do not capitalize short forms used in place of the full name.

Fulton Street	BUT:	**the street**
Empire State Building		**the building**

16. Capitalize the word *city* or *state* only when it is part of the corporate name of the city or state or part of an imaginative name.

Kansas City BUT: **the city of San Francisco**

New York State is called the Empire State.

17. Capitalize *north, south, east, west,* etc., when they designate definite regions or are an integral part of a proper noun.

in the North	**the far North**
out West	**the West Coast**

18. Capitalize such words as *Northerner, Southerner,* and *Midwesterner.*

19. Capitalize *northern, southern, eastern, western,* etc., when these words pertain to the people in a region and to their political, social, or cultural activities. Do not capitalize these words, however, when they merely indicate general location or refer to the geography or climate of the region.

Eastern bankers	BUT: **the eastern half of Pennsylvania**
Southern hospitality	**southern temperatures**

20. Capitalize names of *days, months, holidays,* and *religious days.*

Wednesday **February**

21. Capitalize the names of the seasons only when they are personified.

Come, gentle Spring.

BUT: **Our order for *fall* merchandise was mailed today.**

22. Capitalize the names of historical events and imaginative names given to historical periods.

the American Revolution
the Middle Ages

23. Do not capitalize the names of decades and centuries, such as *the thirties* and *the twentieth century.*

24. Capitalize formal titles of acts, laws, bills, and treaties, but do not capitalize common-noun elements that stand alone in place of the full name.

the Social Security Act BUT: **the act**

25. Capitalize the names of races, peoples, tribes, religions, and languages, such as *Chinese* and *Sanskrit.*

26. Do not capitalize the words *sun, moon,* or *earth* unless they are used in connection with the capitalized names of other planets or stars.

The *sun* was hidden behind a cloud.

In our astronomy class we have been comparing the orbits of Mars, Venus, and *Earth*.

27. Capitalize the names of specific courses of study. However, do not capitalize names of subjects or areas of study, except for any proper nouns or adjectives that are found in such names.

***American History 201* meets on Tuesdays and Thursdays. (Course title.)**

I have decided to major in *American history*. (Area of study.)

28. Do not capitalize academic degrees used as general terms of classification (for example, a *bachelor of arts* degree). However, capitalize a degree used after a person's name (Susan Howard, *Doctor of Philosophy*).

29. Capitalize trademarks, brand names, proprietary names, names of commercial products, and market grades. Do not capitalize the common noun following the name of a product.

Ivory soap **Westinghouse toaster**

30. Capitalize all trade names except those that have become clearly established as common nouns.

Coca-Cola Coke Teflon BUT: **nylon**

31. Capitalize a noun followed by a number or a letter that indicates sequence. EXCEPTIONS: The nouns *line, note, page, paragraph, size,* and *verse* are not capitalized.

Act 1 Class 4 Lesson 20 Policy 3948

32. In titles of literary and artistic works and in displayed headings, capitalize all words with *four or more* letters. Also capitalize words with fewer than four letters except (**a**) articles (*the, a, an*), (**b**) short conjunctions (*and, as, but, if, or, nor*), and (**c**) short prepositions (*at, by, for, in, of, off, on, out, to, up*).

How to Succeed in Business Without Really Trying

"Land Development Proposal Is Not Expected to Be Approved"

NUMBERS

There are two basic number styles in wide use: the *figure style* (which uses figures for most numbers above 10) and the *word style* (which uses figures for most numbers above 100). The figure style is most commonly used in ordinary business correspondence. The word style is used in executive-level correspondence and in nontechnical material.

Figure Style

1. Spell out numbers from 1 through 10; use figures for numbers above 10. This rule applies to both exact and approximate numbers.

We ordered *ten* cases, but they have only *four* or *five* in stock.

Please send us *35* copies of your bulletin.

NOTE: Even the numbers 1 through 10 may be expressed in figures (as in this sentence) when emphasis and quick comprehension are essential. This is the style used in tabulations and statistical matter.

2. Use the same style to express *related* numbers above and below 10. (If most of the numbers are below 10, put them all in words; if most of the numbers are above 10, express all in figures.)

> **Smoke damaged *five* dresses, *eight* suits, and *eleven* coats.**

3. For fast comprehension, numbers in the *millions* or higher may be expressed in the following way:

> **21 million (in place of 21,000,000)**
> **14½ million (in place of 14,500,000)**

a. This style may be used only when the amount consists of a whole number with nothing more than a simple fraction or decimal following. A number such as *4,832,067* must be written all in figures.

b. Treat related numbers alike.

> **Last year we sold 21,557,000 items; this year, nearly 23,000,000.** (NOT: **23 million.)**

Word Style

1. Spell out all numbers, whether exact or approximate, that can be expressed in one or two words. (A hyphenated compound number like *twenty-one* or *ninety-nine* counts as one word.) In effect, spell out all numbers from 1 through 100 and all round numbers above 100 that require no more than two words (such as *sixty-two thousand* or *forty-five million*).

> **We received *twenty-three* letters asking for copies of your speech to our club.**

2. Express related numbers the same way, even though some are above 100 and some below.

> **We mailed *three hundred* invitations and have already received over *one hundred* acceptances.**

3. When spelling out large round numbers, use the shortest form possible.

> **We will need about *twelve hundred* copies.**

4. Numbers in the millions or higher *that require more than two words when spelled out* may be expressed as follows:

> **231 million (in place of 231,000,000)**
> **9¼ billion (in place of 9,250,000,000)**

5. Always spell out a number that begins a sentence, and for consistency, also spell out related numbers.

> ***Forty-six* cartons were shipped today.**
>
> ***Twenty* to *thirty* percent of the goods received were defective.** (NOT: **Twenty to 30 percent.)**

6. If the numbers are large (requiring more than two words when spelled out) or if figures are preferable (for emphasis or quick reference), rearrange the wording of the sentence.

> **The agency received *298* complaints.**
>
> (INSTEAD OF: **Two hundred and ninety-eight complaints were received by the agency.)**

7. Always spell out indefinite numbers and amounts, such as *a few hundred votes* or *thousands of dollars*.

Ordinals

1. Spell out all ordinals (*first, second, third,* and so on) that can be expressed in one or two words.

2. Figures are used to express ordinals in certain expressions of dates, in numbered street names above 10, and occasionally in displayed headings and titles for special effect.

NOTE: Ordinal figures are expressed as follows: *1st, 2d* or *2nd, 3d* or *3rd, 4th, 5th, 6th,* and so on. Do not use an "abbreviation period" following an ordinal.

Dates

1. When the day *precedes* the month or *stands alone,* express it either in ordinal figures (*1st, 12th, 23d*) or in ordinal words (the *first,* the *twelfth,* the *twenty-third*).

Our convention starts on the *25th* of July and ends on the *29th*. (Figure style.)

2. When the day *follows* the month, express it in cardinal figures (*1, 2, 3,* and so on).

on March 6 (NOT: **March 6th or March sixth**)

3. Express complete dates in month-day-year sequence, such as *March 6, 1976.*

4. In United States military correspondence and in letters from foreign countries, the complete date is expressed in day-month-year sequence, such as *15 September 1976.*

5. In legal documents, proclamations, and formal invitations, spell out the day and the year. A number of styles may be used.

May twenty-first
nineteen hundred and seventy-six

6. Class graduation years and well-known years in history may appear in abbreviated form.

the class of '77

Money

1. Use figures to express exact or approximate amounts of money; for example, *$5; about $200.*

2. Spell out indefinite amounts of money; for example, *a few million dollars, many thousands of dollars.*

3. Do not add a decimal point or ciphers to a whole dollar amount when it occurs in a sentence.

We are enclosing a check for *$125* for a three-year subscription.

In tabulations, however, if any amount in the column contains cents, add a decimal point and two ciphers to all *whole* dollar amounts for a uniform appearance.

4. Money in round amounts of a million or more may be expressed partially in words.

$12 million OR: **12 million dollars**
$10½ million OR: **10½ million dollars**

a. This style may be used only when the amount consists of a whole number with nothing more than a simple fraction or decimal following. An amount like *$10,235,000* must be written entirely in figures.

b. Express related amounts of money in the same way.

from $500,000 to $1,000,000

(NOT: **from $500,000 to $1 million**)

c. Repeat words like *million* and *billion* with each figure to avoid misunderstanding.

$5 million to $10 million

(NOT: **$5 to $10 million**)

5. Fractional expressions of large amounts of money should be either completely spelled out or converted to an all-figure style.

one-quarter of a million dollars
OR: **$250,000**

(BUT NOT: **¼ of a million dollars** OR **$¼ million**)

6. For amounts under a dollar, use figures and the word *cents*; for example, *50 cents.*

a. Use the style *$.75* in sentences only if related amounts require a dollar sign.

Prices for the principal grains were as follows: wheat, $1.73; corn, $1.23; oats, $.78; rye, $1.58.

b. Use the symbol ¢ only in technical and statistical matter containing many price quotations.

The new prices for these items are as follows: lag bolts, 11¢; wood screws, 4¢; washers, 3¢; drill bits, 89¢.

7. When using the dollar sign or the cent sign with a price range or a series of amounts, repeat the sign with each amount.

$5,000 to $10,000 10¢ to 20¢

If the term *dollars* or *cents* is to be spelled out, use it only with the final amount.

10 to 20 cents

Measurements

1. Measurements that have a technical significance should be expressed in figures for emphasis or quick comprehension. Spell out measurements that lack technical significance.

This rate applies only to packages that weigh less than *2 pounds*.

BUT: **I've gained another *two pounds*.**

NOTE: Dimensions, sizes, and temperature readings are always expressed in figures.

This office measures *12* by *14 feet*.

2. When a measurement consists of several words, do not use commas to separate the words. The measurement is considered a single unit. The unit of measure may be abbreviated or expressed as a symbol only in technical matter or tabular work.

The parcel weighed *6 pounds 14 ounces*.

I am *6 feet 2 inches* tall.

Fractions

1. A mixed number (a whole number plus a fraction) is written in figures except at the beginning of a sentence.

The cost of raw materials has increased *3¼* times in just two years.

2. A fraction that stands alone (without a whole number preceding) should be expressed in words unless the spelled-out form is long and awkward or unless the fraction is used in technical writing.

one-half the vote
three-fourths of the voters

3. Fractions expressed in figures should not be followed by *st, ds, nds,* or *ths* or by an *of* phrase.

3/200 (NOT: **3/200ths**)

If a sentence requires the use of an *of* phrase following the fraction, spell out the fraction.

three-quarters of an hour (NOT: **¾ of an hour**)

Decimals

1. Always write decimals in figures. Never insert commas in the decimal part of a number; for example, *665.3184368*.

2. When a decimal stands alone (without a whole number preceding the decimal point), insert a cipher before the decimal point unless the decimal itself begins with a cipher. (Reason: The cipher prevents the reader from overlooking the decimal point.)

0.55 inch .06 gram

3. Do not begin a sentence with a decimal figure.

Percentages

1. Express percentages in figures, and spell out the word *percent*.

We give quantity discounts up to *15 percent.*

NOTE: The % symbol is used only in tabulations, business forms, interoffice memorandums, and statistical or technical matter.

2. Fractional percentages *under 1 percent* should be spelled out or expressed in decimals.

one-half of 1 percent OR: **0.5 percent**

3. In a range or series of percentages, the word *percent* follows the last figure only. The symbol %, if used, must follow each figure.

Price reductions range from *20 to 50 percent.* BUT: **from 20% to 50%.**

Periods of Time

1. In general, express periods of time in words.

a twenty-minute wait
in twenty-four months

2. Use figures to express periods of time when they are used as technical measurements or significant statistics (as in discounts, interest rates, and credit terms). Also use figures when the number would require more than two words if spelled out.

an 8-hour day **a note due in 6 months**

Clock Time

1. Always use figures with *a.m.* or *p.m.*

a. The abbreviations *a.m.* and *p.m.* are typed in small letters without spaces.

b. When expressing time "on the hour," do not add ciphers to denote minutes except in tables where other times are given in hours and minutes.

Our store is open from 9:30 a.m. to *6 p.m.*

c. Do not use *a.m.* or *p.m.* unless figures are used.

this morning (NOT: **this a.m.**)

d. Do not use *a.m.* or *p.m.* with *o'clock.*

6 o'clock OR: **6 p.m.**
(NOT: **6 p.m. o'clock**)

e. Do not use *a.m.* or *p.m.* with the expressions *in the morning, in the afternoon, in the evening,* or *at night.* The abbreviations themselves already convey one of these meanings.

at 9 p.m. OR: **at nine in the evening**
(NOT: **at 9 p.m. in the evening**)

f. The times *noon* and *midnight* may be expressed in words alone. However, use the forms *12 noon* and *12 midnight* when these times are given with other times expressed in figures.

The second shift ends at *midnight.*

BUT: **The second shift runs from *4 p.m.* to *12 midnight.***

2. With *o'clock* use figures for emphasis or words for formality.

3. When expressing time "on the hour" without *a.m., p.m.,* or *o'clock,* spell the hour out.

He will arrive at *eight* tonight. (NOT: **at 8 tonight.**)

With Abbreviations and Symbols

Always use figures with abbreviations and symbols.

$25 **90¢** **50%**

No. or # With Figures

1. If the term *number* precedes a figure, express it as an abbreviation (singular: *No.;* plural: *Nos.*). At the beginning of a sentence, however, spell out *Number* to prevent misreading.

We have not yet billed the following invoices: *Nos.* 592, 653, and 654.

***Number* 82175 has been assigned to your new policy.**

2. The symbol # may be used on business forms (such as invoices) and in technical matter.

ABBREVIATIONS

1. Use abbreviations and contractions sparingly.

2. Be consistent. Do not abbreviate a term in some sentences and then spell it out in other sentences.

3. When you do abbreviate, use the generally accepted forms. A number of abbreviations have alternative forms, with differences in spelling, capitalization, and punctuation. Again, be consistent.

4. In sentences, when only the surname is used, spell out all titles except *Mr., Mrs., Messrs., Ms.,* and *Dr.*

***Mr.* Ames will be the guest of *Professor* and *Mrs.* King.**

NOTE: In formal writing, *Dr.* may be spelled out when used with only the surname.

5. Abbreviations of academic degrees require a period after each element in the abbreviation but no internal space.

B.A. **Ph.D.** **LL.B.**

6. The names of radio and television broadcasting stations and the abbreviated names of broadcasting systems are written in capitals without periods and without spaces.

Station KFRC **CBS officials**

7. The name *United States* is often abbreviated when it is part of the name of a government agency. In all other uses, however, it should be spelled out.

U.S. Office of Education OR: **USOE**

8. Geographical abbreviations made up of single initials require a period after each initial but *no* space after each internal period. If the geographical abbreviation contains more than single initials, space once after each internal period.

U.S.A. **U.S.S.R.** **N. Mex.** **N. Dak.**

9. A few common business abbreviations are often typed in small letters (with periods) when they occur within sentences but are typed in all-capital letters (without periods) when they appear on invoices or other business forms.

c.o.d. OR: **COD** **cash on delivery**
f.o.b. OR: **FOB** **free on board**

10. Small-letter abbreviations made up of single initials require a period after each initial but no space after each internal period.

a.m. **p.m.** **f.o.b.**

11. All-capital abbreviations made up of single initials normally require *no periods* and *no internal space.*

RCA **FBI** **IQ** **AT&T**

12. If an abbreviation contains more than single initials, space once after each internal period.

sq. ft. **op. cit.**

13. Each initial in a person's name (or in a company name) should be followed by a period and one space.

Pat T. Noonan **L. B. Anders, Inc.**

Full-Blocked Letter Style

Vigorous, Aggressive
With Subject Line and Open Punctuation

March 6, 19--

Mr. Roger S. Patterson
Western Life Company
2867 East Fourth Street
Cincinnati, Ohio 45202

Dear Mr. Patterson

Subject: Form of a Full-Blocked Letter

This letter is set up in the full-blocked style, in which every line begins at the left margin. A few companies modify it by moving the date to the right, but most firms use it as shown here. Because this style is the fastest to type, it is considered very modern. It is natural, although not necessary, to use "open" punctuation with this style of letter.

This letter also illustrates one arrangement of the subject line, which may be used with any style of letter. Like an attention line, a subject line may be typed with underscores or capitals. In a full-blocked letter, it must be blocked; in other letter styles, it may be blocked or centered. It always appears after the salutation and before the body, for it is considered a part of the body.

Legal firms and the legal departments of companies sometimes prefer to use the Latin terms Re or In Re instead of the English word Subject.

Yours very sincerely

Mary Ellen Smith
Mary Ellen Smith
Reference Department

urs

Blocked Letter Style

The Most Flexible
With Direct Address, Quotation, and Postscript

March 10, 19--

REGISTERED

Mr. Philippe Vargos, Gerente
El Aguila, S.A.
1242 Avenida Insurgentes
Mexico D.F.
MEXICO

Dear Mr. Vargos:

It is current practice in American business letters to display price quotations and similar special data in a special paragraph, like this:

> The paragraph is indented five spaces on both sides and is preceded and followed by one ordinary blank linespace.
>
> If it is necessary to use more paragraphs for the quotation, then a standard single blank line is left between paragraphs.

We indicate the mail service (a double space below the date) only if we are sending the correspondence by some special service, such as "special delivery" or "registered"; and we do so only to get the fact indicated on our file copy of the correspondence.

Yours very sincerely,

David I. Collins
Assistant Director
Bureau of Information
and Public Relations

DIC/urs

P.S. We treat postscripts in the same way that we treat other paragraphs, except that we precede each postscript by "PS:" or "P.S."

Semiblocked Letter Style

Conservative, Executive
With Attention Line and cc Notation

March 7, 19--

Grant, Stone & Company
171 Westminster Street
Providence, RI 02904

ATTENTION TRAINING DIRECTOR

Gentlemen:

For a letter design that is both distinctive and yet standard, try this style: semiblocked (one of the two most popular styles) with the paragraphs indented ten spaces (instead of the usual five).

This letter also shows you an alternative arrangement for the attention line: centered, in all capitals (instead of being blocked at the left margin and underscored). In two regards, however, the use of the attention line is standard: It is accompanied by a "standard" salutation, such as "Gentlemen," "Mesdames," "Ladies," or "Ladies and Gentlemen"; and it is typed above the salutation.

Worth noting also in this letter are the following: (1) positioning the date at the margin, as an alternative to starting it at the center; (2) the use of "standard" punctuation, which calls for a colon after the salutation and a comma after the complimentary closing; and (3) the use of the "cc" notation at the bottom to indicate to whom carbon copies of the letter are being sent.

Yours very truly,

Melissa Cory

Melissa Cory, Director

URS
cc Ms. J. Lambeau
Dr. H. Moon

Simplified Letter Style

The Efficiency Expert's
With Open Punctuation and Full-Blocked Design

March 6, 19--

Mr. Richard W. Parker, Jr.
Humphrey Lumber Company
520 Southwest Park Avenue
Portland, Oregon 97208

THE SIMPLIFIED LETTER

You will be interested to know, Mr. Parker, that several years ago the Administrative Management Society (formerly NOMA) designed a new letter form called the "Simplified Letter." This is a sample.

1 It uses the full-blocked form and "open" punctuation.

2 It contains no salutation or closing. (AMS believes such expressions to be meaningless.)

3 It displays a subject line in all capitals, both preceded and followed by two blank lines. Note that the word "Subject" is omitted.

4 It identifies the signer by an all-capitals line that is preceded by at least four blank lines and followed by one--if further notations are used.

5 It seeks to maintain a brisk but friendly tone, partly by using the addressee's name at least in the first sentence.

Perhaps, Mr. Parker, as some say, this form does not really look like a business letter; but its efficiency suggests that this style is worth a trial, especially where output must be increased.

Ralph E. Jones

RALPH E. JONES, TRAINING CONSULTANT